ASHES OF REVOLT

ASHES OF REVOLT

ESSAYS BY
MARJORIE AGOSIN

WHITE PINE PRESS · FREDONIA, NEW YORK

Publication of this book was made possible, in part, by grants from
the National Endowment for the Arts, the New York State Council on the Arts,
and Wellesley College.

Author's Note
I want to thank Dennis Maloney and Elaine LaMattina for their belief in my work;
Diane Russell-Pineda; Bert B. Lockwood, Jr., editor of the *Human Rights Quarterly*, who
encouraged me to publish these essays; and Cristina da Fonseca who was the first
Chilean to publish my poetry during the dictatorship.

Acknowledgments:
"Anne Frank or the Landscape Unrooted" is from *Dear Anne Frank* ©1994, Azul
Editions, Washington, D.C. Used by permission of the publisher.

"The Dance of Life: Women and Human Rights in Chile" previously appeared in *In A
Public Voice*, The Feminist Press, New York, 1995.

"Vision and Transgression: Some Notes on the Writing of Julieta Kirkwood," previously
appeared in *Reinterpreting the Spanish-American Essay*, ed. Doris Meyer, University of
Texas Press, 1995.

"The Disenchanted Generation" first appeared in *The American Voice*, Vol. 30, 1993.

"How to Speak With the Dead" first appeared in *Agni* 39, Spring 1994.

"Women, Politics, and Society in Chile" first appeared in *Michigan State Working Paper*,
No. 235, March 1993.

Acknowledgements continue on page 183.

Book Design: Elaine LaMattina

Cover Painting: Liliana Wilson Grez.

Manufactured in the United States of America.

ISBN 1-877727-56-3

First printing 1996

9 8 7 6 5 4 3 2 1

WHITE PINE PRESS · 10 VILLAGE SQUARE · FREDONIA, NEW YORK 14063

To the disappeared of Latin America,
so their voices will continue to be heard amid the somber darkness.

To my students at Wellesley College,
who understand that privilege means responsibility.

To Joseph and Sonia, my children.

CONTENTS

INTRODUCTION

Ashes of Revolt as an extraordinary collection of essays with richly diversified themes about the recent history of women's voices in human rights in Latin America. In this volume, Marjorie Agosín has also assumed the task of restoring the lost words of the disappeared while reconstructing the continuing journey of those who seek answers about their missing loved ones. In so doing, the author has written a sensitive and energetic text of poetic prose capable of arousing one's fine-tuned sense of hearing much the same way a bell profoundly reverberates from the top of a valley, placing its multiplicity of tone on every trail and rise. Her writing holds together a circle of human remembrance, creating a stark new language spoken by women. The *desaparecidos* also speak, their words emerging from the rubble of silence and repression left by the recent dictatorships in South America.

This book is also about raw confrontation with the cruelest form of death. But Marjorie Agosín comes from Chile, a place where talking to the dead isn't out of the ordinary. She brings her Jewish heritage to these writings, as well. Her grandmother taught her to speak kindly to the photographs of the dead before going to sleep. Stories of the death camps in Europe were part of the oral tradition of her childhood. In Latin America, where she was raised, it is not unusual to include the names of the dead in daily conversation. Rather than denial, this is an acknowledgement of their continued presence in life. Urns with the ashes of a mother or cousin inside of them are sometimes kept in the busiest room of the house. A friend from Chile once pointed to a small vase on a table in her home, explaining that she was glad to have her brother close to her so she could care for him, even though he had requested that she leave him in the garden.

Despite the author's long-standing familiarity with the dead, she treads into the dwellings of the language of the disappeared with foresight and deliberation. Her questions resonate with critical awareness throughout the book. She asks how she can comfort the dead with a poet's voice. How, she ponders, is one able to utter that which is far too painful to utter? How is it possible to sever a silence which was engendered by the lowest crime committed to the human spirit? What shapes would a lexicon of the vanished take on? How, at last, does an artist of words and finely-honed social commitment reconstruct a verbal memory of the dead if the photo album is sealed with horror? How then, she asks, does any form of human expression re-name the thoughts of a person whose body was violated beyond identity? Restoration and a healing of memory are the self-appointed tasks of Marjorie Agosín and her fellow survivors of the "disenchanted generation" of Chilean writers, so the voices of the disappeared might be heard.

Dictatorships bring on a desolation of speech. Words take on restrictive and horrific significance. Young minds lose the right to think freely. In the aftermath, there is a need to return the stolen words to the voices of the silenced without fear of torture or death. For this reason, Agosín has challenged the transitional government of Chilean president Eduardo Frei, proposing that human rights be part of a new national discourse and public space in order that the government itself does not once again become the prime perpetuator of the disease of amnesia.

Agosín wants her readers to become involved in the individual lives of those who fought against outrageous injustice. She is able to blend the ritual of remembering as taught to her by her grandmother with the multiple registers and tones of common voices which are also universal. *Ashes of Revolt* is not a document which sets down the charts and graphs of a death toll. It is about living, vibrant voices in the face of unlimited fear and repression. It is about singing, despite beatings and angry dogs. We are reminded of the new public voices of women invented out of private pain. These were women who dared to climb over garden walls to search for their disappeared daughters and sons. To do this, they often had to free themselves from the smaller dictatorships functioning within their own homes. They raised the conscience of a nation about the glaring similarity between hidden domestic violence and nationally-mandated violence. They went out to face the dictatorship at large in the world that was Chile, and also Argentina, for many, many years.

This valiant treatise does not forget the silences of other death camps in Latin America and the rest of the world. Agosín is truly a citizen of many countries. The silence and recovery of the voices of Mexico's indigenous people is written here, as is the singular testimonial voice of Guatemalan activist Rigoberta Menchú, along with the words of Argentine journalist and dirty war survivor Jacobo Timmerman. Just as the author gazes into a photograph of Anne Frank, talking to her, befriending her, asking questions that she could never ask, the reader is also invited to look upon the faces of the disappeared and talk to them, listening to the sounds of their recreated languages.

During the seventeen-year dictatorship, despite the fact that artists hands were severed, and poets were banished into desolation or death and sinister devices were applied to their throats, songs were not left unsung in that long country bordered by the Andes mountains and the Pacific Ocean. Verse was still written, sometimes on the back of an invoice from a mine turned prison camp. Paper sacks were used to inscribe prohibited truths. Poetry was recited in public places at the naked risk of life, because to those writers threatened by the violence of silence, writing and existence were one and the same. Because poetry, as Marjorie Agosín so eloquently states, is an act of love.

—Diane Russell-Pineda

ASHES OF REVOLT

MY CITY

I invite you to my city so you can imagine it and discover it along with me the way that street corners of a first love are discovered. Come at daybreak when the men who sharpen knives make raucous and beautiful noises, as if to sharpen their souls in the midst of silence and so much unpredictable fog. These guardians of morning go door to door in familiar neighborhoods. They converse with the maids, gossiping as the sound of savage knives ricochets through my city.

At daybreak women, damp and numb from the cold, sweep up the rubble of greed. This is my city, a city of dawns with the diaphanous clarity of a new day and I say to myself, *Good morning, Chile. Good morning, Santiago.* I walk along huge boulevards, the Macul district with its sleepy houses stained a dark brown hue. I am from Nuñoa, a neighborhood once considered to be the home of aristocrats. Now, it is home to the "financially strapped" middle class. There was a meat market right across the street from my house. It was painted a wrathful blue, and the smell of meat sickened us to the very core. My neighborhood is close to Macul, where Irma Muller's house stands. We were neighbors, then, and didn't know it. It was when I became politically active and was feeling perplexed and downhearted, trying somehow to understand the limits of transgression, that I arrived at Irma's house. I came in pain, slipping through shadows, and she came out of her house, walked towards me, gave me a kiss, and I was filled with the light of understanding. She told me how her son, Jorge, had disappeared from that very house, that very entrance. *Over there, on the patio where the lemon trees grow, there is an almond tree in full bloom. He loved that tree.* So on this spring day I once again sit next to Irma, and like the first rays of a temperate summer, the caressing sun reveals unfamiliar omens to us.

I love Irma very much. Before, we were anonymous neighbors. Now we are allies in the face of pain. Jorge won't see the almond tree bloom this year, and I won't be able to tell him about my daughter, Sonia, or my son, Joseph. This is my city, still haunted by the trappings of fear, still appearing to be surrounded by walls that hold in the emptiness, the silences of fear.

We'll go to the cafés. They are almost empty, but their marvelous aroma is unmistakable. Misha is over there by the threshold, meditating and distant. This is where, silken-haired Bohemians dressed in black, we used to congregate. We knew the songs of Edith Piaf. We read Jean Paul Sartre. We believed in utopia and making love. We were a generation of doers. We kissed in secluded places, and the city was like a bed of flowers, always ready to reveal itself. Every park in Santiago was crowded with couples kissing—as if the very roots of desire—perhaps even the end of the earth—could be found in a kiss. And off in the distance, gypsies were telling our futures...

Then, for the next seventeen years the city resembled a forsaken, lonely woman who sat in the foggy parks listening to the click of blood-thirsty heels as gendarmes dragged women by their hair. One day in the plaza, I saw a woman weeping. Her tears filled the trees, the bushes, and the streets. Couples made love in basements. Everything was clandestine and murky, uncertain and ambiguous in the impending arrival of fear.

In my city's many cemeteries, both the living and the dead roam. In the same place where the well-to-do have magnificent tombs, the poor also rest, exposed to the elements—and at the mercy of the grave diggers and the generous Samaritans of the evening. Here in terrace number twenty-nine lie the people of my generation, those who went to the cafes intending to change the world. They arrived here as anonymous beings, their legs and fingernails mutilated. Sometimes their ears or twisted legs were found, and someone would place them in a small box of exquisite wood and give them a name and a date of remembrance. So many women come to terrace twenty-nine. They bear gifts, candles, music boxes, and shells, so the dead will always feel close to the flowing sounds of the sea. I visit them, too, always asking *How do you talk to the dead?* I don't want them to feel afraid. One must be gentle with them, and most important, never tell them about the amnesia so pervasive in the world. I also visit my grandfather, Joseph Halpern, who lies in a Jewish cemetery two blocks from the main cemetery. As is the Jewish custom, his grave has many tiny stones on it from those who visit him. I always bring him lilies, because they remind him of the Vienna woods.

Salvador Allende's grave lies in a tangled state. It is difficult to read the inscription since, like the graves of Pablo Neruda and his wife, it is covered with gladiolus. The caretakers say that only foreigners visit Allende's grave: the living from my city find it hard to draw close to such memories. It is too painful to remember that the torturers are there in the cafés on the corners of the streets or in the schools. There they are, free and blameless, dreaming the dream of a clear conscience. This is my city, ugly and beautiful, treacherous and gentle, a paradox.

The things I love are here in my city. A wall laden with bougainvillea, a small door which seems to be cast under a spell. There are certain street corners where, as an adolescent, I waited for the sheer excitement of seeing that special boy go by.

Your house is over there, between the mountains, very close to the sky. After so many years I walk toward your house, and you are waiting for me, you, the most precious token of the past. I am not afraid of your hands, hands darkened by the defeat of a lonely man's old age. I do not fear your nightmares of the thousands of overpowering voices that censured you. Here in Santiago, our city, I love you in that same old way, and all I have to do is close my eyes to feel the pleasure of having you near.

My city still amazes me. I discover places untamed, fountains brimming with angels or with little fish with golden heads. I discover a boy completely absorbed in silence watching the afternoon fall away. I love my city and its noises, the rain, those aromas of coffee and coriander. I love the dialogue with the first passerby who says "Buenos Días, Señora" to me, and my response, "Buenos Días, Señor." I feel very glad to be alive, glad my eyes are not covered over, glad I still have my arms and my fingernails. Then, I look at my own hand, and for the first time in this city, I can see it.

I gently stroke eucalyptus trees, my mother's and my grandparent's hands, your hand. It is like a pregnant womb, heavy with furrows. This is my city. In the parks, both the dead and the living deliberate. Yes, you can see them—like the woman in the plaza who has been weeping for seventeen years. Her tears are rivers flowing with orchids and white, flower-covered boats. I love my city.

I am proud of having loved the women who work at the markets, the ones who give away fruit, figs, and chamomile for afflictions of both stomach and soul. These are the women who hid the persecuted. There they are, full of spirit, ready to defy death's crushing heels.

Beggars, men who sharpen knives, my narrow-minded uncles and aunts, all live in this city. And even though they label me an indecipherable communist, I share bread and drink, time-honored customs, true bonds of love, and family ties with them.

I invite you on this journey through many doors, through zones of translucence and fear, through homes, friendly and modest, that move us with their ice-covered stones. This is my city. Here, seated on my father's knee, I learned to read. Here, I came to understand the soul's ambiguous textures. Here I spoke without a voice. This is where I come from, and I would know how to get here even if you blindfolded me. I know the city, and she knows me. My dead friends are here, and I will always come back to them and to the woman who weeps on the bench in the plaza and asks me not to forget. I have learned to imagine her wishes. I visit her in my dreams. This is my city, tenacious, horrible, enchanted—and always, mine.

Translated by Diane Russell-Pineda

NERUDA IN THE SOUL, NERUDA IN ISLA NEGRA

Pablo Neruda's house in Isla Negra was closed by the military dictatorship for seventeen years. It was reopened in January 1990 by the new democratic government.

This time I am delirious as I return to Isla Negra. My feet do not stop on dusky street corners inhabited by those old fears, fears of funerals and of people who did not deserve their shattering deaths. This time I return accompanied by the strange glow of the winter's sun, that soft companion of prisoners who, at the beginning of another day of terror, want only to be caressed by a sympathetic sunbeam. I head for Don Pablo Neruda's house—they refer to him as Don Pablo here, using the title more out of affection than out of respect. The house has been closed, mutilated, hidden in the death-like silence of widows and of mothers who hypnotically search for their children's bodies among the waves. This house, with its immense wooden doors, is like a grand dame who emerged from the sea and offers a welcome filled with the scent of honeysuckle and eucalyptus. A red locomotive anchored in the sandy yard seems to say, "Climb aboard, I invite you on a journey. Come hear the bells, the spirit of the house in the sand."

So, pained and grieving, I enter the house. It is impossible not to remember the ones who died of torture during seventeen years of dictatorship, the ones in exile, children born on foreign soil who perhaps, like myself, prepare to return. And soon their feet, like so many orphans, will walk on Isla Negra, a magical site for Don Pablo, the winged heart of his poetry of water.

Inside the house, the harmony created by the sun fills every corner. This house of stone was built in sections with the money Neruda made from the sale of *Cantos General*. The house still belongs to Pablo and Matilde; one can feel their presence. A friendly guide shows us a bedroom that is a vision of watery windows and a large bed next to the sea. The sea, the root of sleep, is a visitor that is always welcome in the hours of vigil, in waking caresses, but more than anything, the sea is an accomplice to immense, deep love. The wooden room warmed by small salamanders and ancient bathtubs silently reflects Pablo and Matilde's desires.

As we move downward from Pablo and Matilde's room. I remember the story of a bird that could reach both the sky and the bottom of the ocean. We reach the living room where Neruda's friends, whose names are carved on the ceiling's beams, used to gather. Neruda's dear friends now accompany us. In the living room there are only a large glass table supported by piano legs, old nautical compasses, and ships in bottles, but the room is filled with silence and memory. At the very end of the room are some beautiful women with faces of water. They are figureheads, including the famous María Celeste, brought from the sea and from distant lands to preserve the stories of Isla Negra. I greet her for the first time. I have seen her before in books and have read poems about her. Now I approach her, and as we look at each other, we learn to cry.

Beyond the living room and the permanent presence of Neruda's friends, we spread out through narrow and mysterious halls until we reach the collection room. The room still awaits the arrival of Neruda's well-travelled shells. The poet donated them a long time ago to the University of Chile, where the infamous bureaucracy locked them up, never even cataloging these multicolor, mysterious baubles that hold the secrets of so many lives.

In addition to collecting words, Neruda collected things, but not with the astute eye of a collector or professional. He liked simple, magical things, like teacups, plaster ears, locomotives, pipes, butterflies, and, of course, rare books. Displayed in his collection room are miniature pipes and blue bottles that filter the light of the sun and sea, giving off a colored texture, almost ghostly but beautiful. The hand and look Neruda cast on all his possessions were not those of a collector, but of a poet and lover of all things.

In one of the last rooms in this house that unfolds like a great labyrinth near the sea is a plaster horse that was burned in one of Chile's earthquakes. The horse is large and sweet, a big kid's toy. It then occurs to me that Don Pablo had to build a room especially for this horse, something any poet would understand.

I am both happy and confused. Each room is occupied by odors of a long and shared happiness. I imagine Don Pablo at his desk in the small house "La Cobacha," which hangs above the ocean, where he wrote every day in his enormous notebooks in green ink, inspired by poetry and the sea. I close my eyes to recall when I was a child, and Don Pablo gave me a honeysuckle. I also see him prostrate with a debilitating cancer, asking Matilde and his friends to leave him for the last time in the soul of the winter ocean.

I contemplate that same ocean this afternoon, and it reminds me of life. I think of Isla Negra and the fact that Neruda's house is now open to the public, so children can meet the giant horse with its golden tail. I remember Isla Negra, asleep, pillaged, and silenced for seventeen years. The giant doors to Don Pablo's house were padlocked by deranged military officers. Now the enormous bell sways with the softness of a mother rocking a child to sleep. The island celebrates Chile's new democracy. I see that Isla Negra is not just Don Pablo Neruda's town. It belongs to all of us, because it is now free, and the house in the sand, occupied by bells, sun, and time, is still inhabited by its omnipresent owners.

Translated by Janice Molloy

In the fog I remember

On the coastal regions of my country we can go deeply into long trails and cross shadowy rock-bound land formations, treading like sleepwalkers with the overpowering presence of the Pacific Ocean in our eyes. And the fog that covers the thick air wraps itself around us until it makes us disappear, turning us into outlines and blurry ghosts with lost faces. I ponder this image and associate it with memory which is fragile and vanishing and yet becomes transparent when it is recreated. Then, we are human beings once more and return to our beginnings.

I grew up in Chile. A country which was for centuries a refuge for fugitives and exiles, it is a place filled with ghosts and memories. My grandparents crossed several oceans: the Black Sea, the Mediterranean, and then reached the Pacific ocean. They spoke foreign languages, Russian and Turkish, and when they wanted to remember their ancestral lineage, they covered up the mirrors.

My grandparents escaped the pogroms and theNnazi Holocaust. We are part of South America's history. We are bound to it because it gave us refuge and allowed us to live in freedom. When we arrived at its ports of entry, South America greeted us with gestures of love

My paternal grandparents came from Odessa, to the small village of Quillota, in the central valley, a place known for its avocados and *chirimoyas* (a soft, succulent, green and white fruit). There, they continued that wise and ancient craft of tailoring, which they had learned in faraway Russia, because it was the only skill they were allowed to pursue in order to survive. And so, by using their needles, they were able to stitch their story together and to tell it. And that is how, in their last days, they were finally able to become benevolent and illustrious citizens.

My grandparents believed in giving. They were generous with animals, and always gave them the best meat. They also helped nuns and refugees, and gave them the best cloth. In southern Chile, my maternal grandfather gave shelter to refugees from Nazi Germany. Within that setting, I grew up with the conviction that a citizen is someone who is noble and solidary, one who is responsible to his or her fellow human beings.

My childhood in Chile was magical and happy. In our school, we placed great importance on poetry. We read it out loud. We had poetry clubs, and we venerated Gabriela Mistral, that unpretentious school teacher who won the Nobel prize for literature and bought shoes for the poor. She and Neruda were our heroes.

We enjoyed literature, stories, and fables. And for the most part, our understanding of words was linked to orality, to non-written forms of communication and to conversations which lasted until the wee hours of the morning. It is often said that Latin Americans waste time in cafés, talking and drinking together. Leisure time however, is a wonderful way to analyze the world, passions and tokens of love. My culture is molded out of conversations between my parents' and my grandparents' generations. We shared life intensely. And we are drawn together by a historic destiny to communicate with one another because we are a remote country divided between the mountain ranges and the ocean. That is why we are characterized as both shy and hospitable people.

The art of leisure conversation with a glass of wine or a cup of coffee, became one of our traits. Years later, at college, when we had reached the age of idealism we, with our black dresses and sophisticated cigarettes, longed to change the world. I belonged to a wonderful generation of students who made an effort to spend their summers working for literacy campaigns in the rural areas of Chile. They read philosophy, recited the poetry of Mistral, and read Jean Paul Sartre and Beauvoir.

During the 1970's, Chilean universities were ebullient, noisy, political centers. Grades did not concern us in the least. However, political ideology, or what we called justice, did, and we sometimes forgot our meager political preferences.

I do not idealize this moment in time; rather, I approach it with caution. I do not wish to transform the people of my generation into heroes, but I believe that perhaps we were. In the same way that my grandparents survived the pogroms and the Holocaust, and found peace in Chile, my generation witnessed a tumultuous era of tragic political consequences. In 1970, Chile became the first socialist country to elect a Marxist president, Salvador Allende. That evening, the people who lived in the outskirts of the city danced on the sidewalks, and women gave away freshly-cut flowers from the fields. They also participated in that festival of emotions with huge, non-threatening flags that surrounded the city. In another section of the city, a different Chile remained in silence and in the shadows.

The Socialist experiment only lasted for two years, but it turned us into a socially committed generation. We were committed to the young, toothless women who worked in the public markets, to the illiterate and the sick. Despite the fact that certain sectors of the socio-political hierarchy have always been opposed to change, in those two short years, the spirit of Chile was transformed into a fervent and unified society.

The Pinochet years (1973-1987) were filled with unspeakable horrors. However, in the midst of tremendous hostility, mistrust, and hate, human dignity grew. Dictatorships are not merely people with knives and huge boots, like characters in fairy tales. Rather, they rely upon skillfull destroyers of society and communication. They made us drink the wine of loneliness in exchange for the din and joy of the cafés and forced us to exist in a permanent state of mistrust, fear, and silence.

When the dictatorship came to my country, I was twenty-five. Some of my friends disappeared. No one ever heard about them again. It was as if they had left for the shore, and the dense fog had taken them away from any possibility of life or future. Some of them immigrated to Europe and the United States and became nomads and exiles. I didn't want to leave my country. I was happy in Chile, I didn't speak English, and I loved my school, my pens and pencils, my notebooks, the trees, the sky, and my grandmother, Josefina. But we left, and I was to repeat the story of another exile, this time for political reasons. We left Chile to be free. We came to the United States, where I had to learn a new language, where making friends was awfully hard. I survived nonethless, because in my mind I was able to invent my country, that land lost between the mountains and the sea. I would write letters, listen to music, and read poetry. All of this saved me from the terrible fear of being someone without a memory or a woman without a history or a country.

During the years of the military dictatorship, my political conscience and my desire to exercise the privilege of speech intensified with my involvement in human rights projects, especially those concerning women, the social group which had suffered the most. From far away, I joined groups that brought together women from Chile, Argentina, and Guatemala who were searching for their sons and daughters. I had no desire to be heroic, but the complicity of silence was horrifying to me. We were brave more out of necessity than choice.

In Latin America, ninety thousand young people disappeared. They left their homes carrying books. They had no guns or grenades, only flowers. And they disappeared. Their mothers remember them, but they have no graves where they can go to talk to them, and they don't know when or where they died. Many of the mothers remember and observe the anniversary of the death of their children on the day they were taken away. These are anniversaries of loneliness, filled with empty places at the table. The death camps in Yugoslavia unmistakably remind us of the ashes at Auschwitz. In Ruanda, knives remind us of every dictatorship, of the broken fragments of the human spirit, and of the fragility of the soul. So we ask ourselves, Why live? What can we do? Where can we live? In what direction can we flee? And yet, certain circumstances bring us closer to the human spirit and to the life-breath of solidarity.It is better to open a door than to live in darkness. It is better to think about poetry and become energized than to fabricate a lexicon of violence, hostility, and the devaluation of those who are defenseless.

Chile was saved by an infinite number of heroic deeds, both great and small. It was saved because when the gendarmes appeared with tear gas, a door suddenly opened and someone offered shelter. When the police held back the people with gigantic clubs, somone offered his or her hand to a frightened woman. Together, they created alliances, overcame fear, and someone offered a rose to a prison warden.

From her hideaway, Anne Frank continued to believe that people were good. That belief, more than innocent optimism, holds within it the possibility of a future, the possibility of saying no to terror, and a faith in the human spirit.

In Chilean prisons, men and women wrote poems or made beautiful sculptures crafted out of rocks from remote islands. The mothers of political prisoners embroidered sackcloth tapestries in order to inscribe their true stories. These simple tapestries, made from worn-out pieces of cloth, travelled all around the world to tell the story of a country held captive behind barbed wire.

I tell you this story so that you will not forget them, and don't forget me either. I am also a product of crossings and exiles. It began that day when my grandfather, Joseph, stepped off the boat in the port of Valparaíso to later save my grandmother, Helena, from the death camps, and continued when, at the height of the dictatorship, my father saved me and I left Chile.

We left Chile one year before the military dictatorship began. I endured, but I also lost roots, my friends, and my language. Nevertheless, I didn't care to be like those lost souls on that foggy morning coast. I became an ally of the victims and those who had no voice. Bureauocrats and the military have always seemed hateful to me. I had no desire to be heroic or famous. I wanted only to be one more in the endless tangle of possibilities. I did not want to hide in the fog and lose the right to rescue memory. I endured, I spoke, and I continue to believe in men and women who are good.

Translated by Diane Russell-Pineda

ALWAYS FROM
SOMEWHERE ELSE:
REFLECTIONS ON EXILE

My father, Moisés Agosín, whose very name evokes exodus, landed in Chile in 1926 aboard a fragile craft for refugees and dreamers. He was born in Marseilles, though his parents were Russian Jews who had fled the pogroms of Czar Nicholas. Exile, always being from somewhere else, feeling separate and different, is still an essential part of my history and my identity. My grandparents on my father's side spoke Russian, French, and Turkish since they had spent three years in Istanbul prior to arriving in Marseilles.

People say history moves in cycles, repeats itself, but it is also filled with mysterious chance occurences, unforeseeable coincidences. My own exile was part of a family tradition linked to the vagabond fate of the Jewish people. I also suffered exile, but I didn't travel in a cargo ship across the Atlantic to the Pacific. We crossed vast expanses in an airplane that reminded me of a mischievous bird turning pirouettes in the sky. Back then, I was an adolescent who loved the Beatles, black clothes, Neruda's poetry, and my country, Chile.

In 1974, one year after the military coup that overthrew President Salvador Allende, my parents decided to go into exile, to leave their country and our extended family in order to live in freedom. They left so that we would not have to attend universities controlled by the military or have to ask permission every time we wished to get together with more than three people at a time.

We left Chile one beautiful September day. The myrrhs, those lovely bushes of the Southern Hemisphere, were in bloom, yellow, like butterflies suspended in the air. I gazed nostalgically at the Andes, splendid and majestic, and I recalled that my mother's parents had crossed them by mule from the Argentine border. Now I joined them, joined that history of a pilgrimmage, this time not for being a Jew but for being a socialist. Just as my grandparents arrived in Chile in search of political and religious refuge, my parents, my brothers, and I, nearly half a century later, abandoned that country which had opened its doors to so many immigrants during the two world wars.

Now we, too, were searching for the peace and freedom of expression all refugeees long for, but with the difference that my parents belonged to an intellectual elite and we were headed for a powerful country: the United States. When I got there, I did not know how to speak English, and learning was a painful and lonely venture. My classmates in the public school of Athens, Georgia made fun of me. They called me "Jew" and "Latina." (In the early 1970s, multiculturalism was not yet in fashion.) I couldn't defend myself or even speak at all. Though I had left behind the censors of my own country, I found myself silenced once again—in a democrcy! Since the United States was responsible for the military coup that overthrew the government of Salvador Allende, I felt as though I were living in the country that had betrayed my own. Because of that, and of my scanty knowledge of English, I grew quiet. For a long time, I lived in expanses of silence that bit by bit were transformed into the texts of my poems.

In my adolescence in Georgia, I began to write long letters to my girlfriends, asking about the weather, certain flowers, fragrances, certain streets. I wanted to reconstruct all I had lost and all I longed for: my house, my grandparents' garden, the smell of the food, my friends' giggles when they talked about love. The writer in exile tries to recreate what has been drastically lost. Memory becomes her most precious ally, as well as her most disturbing obsession.

These letters allowed me to stay in direct contact with my language, with my history. Later such epistles grew into long poems that evoked the land, the longed-for country, but the political drama of Chile was also present. The experience of exile and the historical context of my departure became the central focus of my writing. Were it not for the military coup of 1973, I would not have written poetry about the blindfolded and disappeared, about the pain of nameless bodies buried in common graves. I wrote obsessively because I could not forget. Nor did I wish to because by writing about a darkened continent, I also reconstructed my own history and my flight. My only possible return was through words.

Just as language was censored, usurped in the nations of the Southern Cone in the 1970s and 1980s, in my exile language became my only possibility of freedom, of touching my history, my country, my identity. Words brought me closer to that memorable natural world of Chile, to clandestine conversations, and it allowed me to say the unsayable. I was in exile, and I could dare to say what could not be said there, in the South. But I always wondered: For whom do I say the unsayable? I wrote in Spanish and always had to rely on a faithful translator to tell my story so that readers could understand something of the mothers who clutched photographs of their loved ones to their breasts and asked, "Where are they?"

The writer in exile writes for an audience of remote phantoms. I wrote to say something about that gagged place called Chile, about the silence and indifference of people who succumbed to the demons of fear. But I also wrote for a U.S. audience who, though untouched by that fear, felt solidarity and sought to understand those stories of repression and pain. My status as a Chilean writer in exile and living in the United States was, and continues to be, problematic. Desite the fact that a large number of Latin American intellectuals and writers emigrated to the United States in the 1970s, we were always a small and islolated minority. Except for me and people like Ariel Dorfman and Isabel Allende, who wrote for a mass market, Chilean writers wrote for themselves, for each other, and for those interested in exile. Though we became members of the intellectual community in the United States, I suspect our experience was not really of interest to many, especially from 1973 to 1977.

I didn't take part in Latino movements in the U.S., such as those of Chicanos and Puerto Ricans. We Latin American writers, especially those of us from the Southern Cone, had a radically diffeerent experience from those born in the United States. Our political ideology was also different. Besides, because we appeared to be an elite, we were not always accepted by Latinos in the United States. Those who wrote in English built alliances and made names

MARJORIE AGOSIN

for themselves, but those of us who were in thrall to the trauma of exile and the unceasing chimera of return could not, nor did we wish to, integrate ourselves into a multicultural and multifaceted community. We lived immersed in our history, in our cultural heritage, quite apart from that of Latino writers, and perhaps we never emerged from that status. When we were introduced, it was as writers in exile, as if exile were a temproary illness or an ID card.

For many writers of my generation and the one that came before, exile became a subject that defined us, marked us, as if that experience were the only true sign of identity. Some wrote obsessively about the pain of living the loss of a community, the loss of contact with ancestral roots. Some writers turned that pain into a tourist attraction, made for export. Their books were easy sentimental reads rather than demanding reflections on the pain of loss that went beyond an individuals's concerns.

Although obsessed, I did not take part in the tourism of pain, nor did I fall into doing agitprop poetry barely respectful of the subject. My books, *Las zonas del dolor* (Zones of Pain), *Círculos de la locura* (Circles of Madness), and my recent *Una cruz y una estrella, reminiscencias de una niña jukdâ en Chile* (A Cross and a Star: Reminiscences of a Jewish Girl in Chile) all allude to living on the edge of the historical circumstances in which the writer finds herself. I wrote about Chile's prisons, about faces tattooed by torture, their gazes vague and silent. Distance helped me to recreate my memory, to invent a Chile that was different from the one others lived, a Chile of myth, a Chile invented through distance.

My exile was like the one that Homer describes in the *Odyssey*: a form of disappearance, of ceasing to exist in the familial setting of memory, of ceasing to be part of the great clan of family alliances. I left, disappeared, and joined the nameless generations of those born between 1950 and 1955, humans moved by utopian dreams who tried to transform Chilean society in the 1970s, many of whom then disappeared without leaving a trace of young bodies once filled with life. Only a few write now about those who died—or even invoke their memory. Only their relatives remember them. I am one of a few women writers in exile who, as a form of survival, write about that lost generation, about those young people who made the revolution with pencils and poems. I write by their side, and I name them again and again, not for the tourism of pain but for the hope of rescuing their memory, reinventing it, making it my own and everyone's, raising the consciousness of future generations in Chile and elsewhere.

For years I thought my poems and essays were written for the inhabitants of my far-off country, that somehow my writing belonged to them. But exile also gave me the power to exist in many lands, on thousands of borders, in many languages. The experience of being a Southern cone writer in exile allowed me to become universal, to become an ally, as well, of the mothers who search for their children in El Salvador, in Guatemala. I could write about Anne Frank because she, like my generation, was robbed of the right to live and be happy.

Gabriela Mistral was a perpetual exile and traveler who, in numerous poems and letters, alluded to the fact that to live outside your own country is to live without happiness. Without the intuitive familiarity of things, I would add, such as certain noises that put us to sleep very early in the immensity of the night and that awaken us in the softness of the morning. To live in exile is to lose the familiarity of your own face and walk the streets of foreign cities without being recognized by anyone. For a writer, exile is the solitude that is imposed in the house of memory, the mirrors we carry aound inside.

Writers in exile can go back to their countries when democracy returns, and many have done so. But others, though they try, find they cannot, and still others do not even want to try. Exiled writers get insidious and satirical comments from those who think they lived like heroes in their adopted countries. No one thinks about the poor neighborhoods where they lived, the restaurants where they waited on tables, or whether they had difficulties with the language.

I have discovered that return implies another exile. The mythical Chile of my childhood, the Chile of my early adolescence and of the student Bohemia has disappeared. The Chile of my parents has vanished. We Chileans today are concerned with feeding our children, with getting the basics to survive. We were once a generation of poets and dreamers, but we lost our lives in prisons or in clandestine jails. And we also lost our lives in exile.

Both the writer in exile and the one who stayed behind were subjected by the dictatorship to a heart-rending silence, to a culture of fear, to writing in secret self-imposed codes, and to existing in the sacred no-man's land where reading is considered a subversive act. Both the exile and the one who stayed behind lived in a dangerous and foggy place, where every word could be a metaphor. Those who stayed behind had to translate their work into the language of secret codes, the writer's accomplice. And those, like me, who left, were catalogued as foreign writers, exiles who need to be translated not only literally but in varying contexts and shades.

For me, returning to Chile is fraught with conflict. The Chile of Salvador Allende is but a myth of the past, the now-quelled dream of my parents that only exists in the memory of those who—shuttered in their homes in exile—listened to Violeta Parra, drank *pisco,* and gave their children a persistent longing for their lost country.

My children were born in the United States, but they speak Spanish; they like *empanadas,* and periodically they visit their great-grandmother on my mother's side, the same great-grandmother who crossed the Andes on the back of a mule and survived ancestral wanderings. My children love that country where my childhood was magical, with colorful rocks and poets walking its shores. I tell them about these things I lived, and perhaps I am repeating what my parents did when they told me there was a country called Chile, so far away that it seemed like a star at the end of the world.

During these long years outside Chile, I have lived in a space where borders vanished, where writing is not so tied to place since it includes a larger community of human beings. The possibility of being translated into English has opened new doors. I think of myself as being from a long, narrow and far-off country but also as being from everywhere. When I go back to Chile, people call me *"la gringa,"* or they say, "You're from there now." When I am in the United States, they tell me, "It must be so sad to leave your country and be a foreigner." Such comments are part of my reality, a hybrid complex reality, a bicultural and bilingual reality caught between two countries, two languages, and two heritages—Christian and Jewish.

My grandparents' wanderings helped me to feel comfortable in foreign lands. I carry my father's name, Moisés, like a solid metaphor of the lives of these travelers. Judaism, which was always something uncomfortable for Chilean society, especially the upper class, has allowed me to feel comfortable in the diluted and foggy zones of nations and borders. It seems that I am always prepared to leave somewhere, taking with me the only possible homeland: language, memory, the invention of it. But I also think that even if they blindfolded me in the dark, I would find my way back to Chile.

Translated by Mark Fried

ANNE FRANK
OR THE
LANDSCAPE UPROOTED

Growing up beside the voices of my great-grandmothers, who had escaped Vienna and Odessa, I learned early on to value the importance of remembrance. My great-grandmother Helena, marked by the specters of war, often recalled the moment she escaped her house in Vienna under the heavy cloak of night, frightened and crippled, and how suddenly there appeared a reddish star that showered radiance upon her, and right then she knew that she could begin to envision a better destiny.

Many years later, when I left my native Chile because of the fascist military dictatorship, I carried with me in a small plastic bag a clump of earth, and in that earth I had planted a gardenia so I'd remember its fragrance always.

Memory has an indelible way of selecting what from the past is timeless and sacred. My own childhood memories are filled with certain fragrances, silences, certain thresholds opening and closing. In my house in Santiago there were certain photographs that kept me good company, that watched over me like a constant presence. There were photographs of my great-grand-father Isidoro, whom we named the chocolate-covered soldier because he was so beautiful and exquisite; also there was a photograph of my aunt Emma who sang arias and spoke French; and there was a small photograph of Anne Frank that my grandfather José had given me in the summer of 1970.

We children of the house would look at those photographs filled with a sense of awe and mystery. My great-grandmother Elena would kiss them every night before going to bed, especially her chocolate-covered soldier to whom she was married during so many agonizing days of war, and her sister Emma whom she sought out for sound advice and old recipes. Every night she would take leave of them, reassured, because the next day she would repeat this same eccentric, sacred ritual. I now realize that with those photographs my great-grandmother was reviving the memory of her loved ones, offering them a final resting place, a place in which to be remembered, a visible epitaph.

My grandmother Helena had understood the importance of preserving remembrance as one's most precious possession. Living in a predominately Catholic country, she carried on the Jewish tradition of lighting the Sabbath candles, guarding a profound peace in which to remember her dead. Also, in those rare private moments when she thought she wouldn't be disturbed, she would devote herself to building little altars with the meager objects she had brought with her from Europe's war-torn cities.

Anne Frank's presence in that little photograph was always at my side during my childhood nightmares. I knew that Anne had written a diary and that she had perished in the concentration camps only months before the arrival of the Allied Forces. There was something in her face, in her aspect, and her age that reminded me of myself. I imagined her playing with my sisters and reading fragments of her diary to us. Curiously, Anne Frank's face became an unusual presence in my life, not so much because this Jew had become a historic and religious symbol, but because she had a name, had a face, because she wasn't just one more anonymous story among the countless stories of the Holocaust. Anne invites us to think of her simply as a girl in adolescence, a girl filled with desires to love and to rage. In her diary, she talks about her relations with her parents and her sister, and all the others forced to live in that secret annex. Elsewhere in her diary she mentions what she desires most after liberation: how she longs to eat pastry or live in a house that is roomy, clean and bright. These are Anne's desires, the marks of an ordinary everyday life.

That surviving photograph of Anne Frank continues today to illumine every corner of the globe in sharp contrast to those perfectly preserved images of "The Final Solution," where the human body takes on the horrific physiognomy of the unspeakable. Sometimes I would ask myself how she might have looked with her head shaven, and then I'd recall her eyes and her gaze that seemed to look out from the very depth of things. Anne Frank has left us a human face, a human body, and it is precisely that humanness that the families of the victims try to preserve, be it with photographic altars or by means of remembrance that speaks the soul's language, that sees from within, that questions and exclaims.

I began my dialogue with Anne Frank from a simultaneous desire to remember and to forget. I wanted to know more about that curious girl's face that for so long had occupied a place on the wall of my room. I invoked her presence from a deep desire to forget her as a martyr and, instead, to present her with all the tribulations of a thirteen-year-old girl. I wanted to ask her; Why did you believe that men were truly good? Why did you have so much faith in the power of writing? How did you love so much in the darkness of that secret annex? How did you remain so high-spirited and full of joy?

I wanted to speak with Anne Frank from an almost obsessive desire to revive her memory and make her return and enter our daily lives. I needed to ask: What would we have done if Anne Frank came to our door and asked us to hide her, asked us to lodge her for one night or ten years?

Ultimately, all the writings about the Holocaust, and in particular one book entitled *The Rescuers*, urge us to rethink the moral character of those citizens who were wrapped in the shroud of ignorance and indifference, those civilian accomplices to a relentless and merciless brutality. What would a Christian mother in Amsterdam have done if Anne Frank had begged her for a piece of bread? Would she have closed the door on her to maintain the perfect order of her family and home?

While civil disobedience, saying no to the authoritarian forces of the Nazis, had no doubt played an integral part in saving the lives of the persecuted, still the timeless and unanswerable question remains: Why did so many people submit and obey?

Anne Frank's diary forces us to re-evaluate the relationship between the everyday present, the past and the concept of nationhood. Holland was one country that openly declared its solidarity with its Jewish citizens and where the greatest number of Jews were rescued. But even so, Amsterdam was the city in which the most Jews were murdered because the flat openness and easy accessibility of the landscape did not permit safely hiding them.

Must nations possess a confounding, unrestrained geography to save human life? What must the moral fabric of nations be like to avoid holocausts and genocide? What is it that causes people to refuse to obey the forces of demagoguery? The diary makes us think concretely about our relationship with the national identity and landscape. Nearly all of Europe obeyed the Germanic call, with only a small minority of European countries hiding and protecting Jews, thus giving rein to the systematic extermination of six million Jews.

Anne Frank was banished and condemned by a collective amnesia of silence and terror. During the transfer of victims to the death camps, people silently stood by and watched as distant, removed observers, as if the gasping bodies of the victims marked off zones of the unspeakable and unimaginable. Anne Frank's diary confronts us directly with history's transformations and postulates the human tragedy of nationalism and the contemptible legacy of racism that remains today a powerful weapon used to divide people and lead them down hatred's path.

My dialogue with Anne Frank also raises questions that have to do with the dictatorships of Latin America's extremist right, and particularly that of my native country, Chile. Like the victims of Nazi genocide, the victims of the genocide committed by Latin America's dictatorships in the '70s did not have places of remembrance where they could be buried, and their families still do not know where to go visit them, to remember them and to offer them life's gifts. The victims of the Holocaust perished in the blue gas chambers, exterminated, deformed beyond recognition. The victims of military dictatorships just disappeared like transfigured, nocturnal ghosts. We are left asking: How can we remember a people who are without graves? This is the same question put forth by the Mothers of the Disappeared. Where does one go to place flowers over their faces, over their bodies eternally asleep somewhere in the air? What is the cathartic ceremony by which to remember them?

In countries like Israel, citizens preserve their memory by means of planting trees, organically linking remembrance with the sun, water and the earth, which are the sources of all life. In Israel there is a forest dedicated to the life and memory of Anne Frank. On the Avenue of the Just, in the most moving of the memorials of the Holocaust, Yad V'shem, brightly illuminated human faces appear amidst intermittent rows of trees, endowing those specters of death with veracity and the breath of life.

Today in Latin America there are as yet no living memorials or monuments dedicated to a whole lost generation, to the thirty thousand disappeared in Argentina alone, and to the ninety thousand murdered and disappeared throughout the rest of Latin America. Nevertheless, the living do remember them. The mothers of the disappeared continue to march, with their hands raised high, in Argentina, in Chile, in Guatemala, in El Salvador.

Anne Frank's diary was first published in 1952. In the history books about the Second World War and the Holocaust, it is appallingly shocking that those statements that attract the most attention are those made by "observers" or "passers-by," by accomplices who assure us that it was possible in the streets and cities—where during the night screams and fists pounding on doors and walls were heard—to not know that the concentration camps existed, far removed from the world's view. Today, those screams are still heard in the cities of Latin America and in what was once the Republic of Yugoslavia.

For many years Anne Frank's diary stayed on my night table. Often I dreamed of her and wanted to comfort her, to promise her that Europe, after the ashen deluge, would be a beautiful, clean and clear place. In 1973, when Chile's military junta smashed down the doors of our neighborhood to arrest the women, yanking them off by their hair that would later be shaven off; when they disappeared them on dense foggy nights, I thought about Anne Frank. When the military junta in Argentina tortured Jews under portraits of Hitler, I thought about Anne Frank.

But we must not hold Anne Frank up as a saintly or mythical figure, not even as a heroic figure for having been the victim of Nazi genocide. We must look to Anne Frank for her religious and political tolerance, as well as for her unshakable ability to feel amazement and outrage in the face of beauty and horror. At the same time that she tells us how women and children were carried off pitilessly before the indifferent eyes of fearful passers-by, she also tells us that she still believes in the nobility of the human spirit and the dignity of man.

Anne Frank is not an icon in any official Jewish history; she was a young girl who wasn't able to live out the fullness of adolescence, whose chance for happiness was cruelly snatched away, who was denied the right to live. Her diary, beyond being a personal memoir, is the public and collective account of a history that made itself heard. Her diary compels us to face up to the past, to our own history in the making, and to the future of history.

Monuments and memorials can only attempt to rescue from oblivion the memory of the dead, of invisible women and men, by offering them an honored place in history. But a diary that can be read out loud, as personal testimony and oral history, allows us to feel the power of giving human voice to the process of memorializing history. Anne Frank's diary makes us think about the way in which we've managed to remember the past and how we respond to that past in our future actions. Even after so many years and after so much travel over endless crossroads, I still keep very close to me that little photograph of Anne Frank passed on to me by my grandfather, a Viennese Jew living in Santiago de Chile, and that I will one day pass on to my children.

Translated by Richard Schaaf

A Dream of Shadows:
Writing, Speaking, Becoming

To speak of language, of joining words to make of them a text, of reweaving them to form new designs, and plotting new ways for being and living are the tools of my vocation. In childhood, rather than gliding down slides, I liked to repeat the sounds of words. In my mind, I would hear them resonant and clear, round to the touch as I languidly caressed them with my naive tongue. Sometimes, saying forbidden words gave me an immense pleasure, and the mere act of thinking them would lead me down the road of transgression. Words and my desire to use them have been an abundant and constant source for me in my work, from the very first moment I began to respond to the obsessive rhythms of writing.

In the course of my childhood, I filled up with words, words shared with my generous nannies—the proud women who devote their lives to caring for Latin America's privileged daughters. My nannies used to sing me lullabies. Instead of lulling me to sleep, their songs made me more aware of language in its most rudimentary physicality. Through the songs of these women, I gathered the first token of speech, of whispering, of the silent language that is more familiar to women than to men.[1]

My writing developed with the whispering of the women who inhabited the back rooms—the servants' quarters. In the afternoon, when it rained, we sat in those dark rooms listening to the soap operas on the radio. We cried and became infuriated, and we talked while we listened to the mishaps of the protagonists, who were usually underprivileged victims of systems that either favored one class above others or were based on a patriarchal hierarchy.

As I listened to these soap operas and to my nannies singing next to the stove with its intermittent glow and heard the women tell stories they reelaborated and reinvented with every telling, my deepest self came closer to the process of writing in this oral, lively, audacious and feminine incipience. We women are much closer to the expressions of daily life, not necessarily due to our zeal for domestic things, but because we are used to feeling, to sensing language in its varied manifestations: from the gestation of the word, from the rocking of the cradle lulling us with speech rhythms–the language not yet captured by "the father"–to the oral tradition.

My literary space was conditioned in the back rooms, beside the women who practiced their way of speaking in underprivileged spaces–spaces behind closed doors, occupied by their silence, modesty, and obedience. My approach to the "underprivileged" was not an easy endeavor. It was my vocation and my profession. It was not anything I planned but rather the result of intuition and a sense of loyalty to them.

From an early age, from the first attempts at writing poetry that makes evident the ability to plot and lucubrate, my writing became nestled in images that sprang from the deepest recesses. Writing was for me a two-sided game: Being able to speak and knowing when to keep silent; when to measure words and when to dream up new ones. For these reasons, the traps of Sor Juana– the deceiving tactics: pretending not to say what must be said– or "the traps of the weak," as Josefina Ludmer refers to them in Sor Juana's response to Filotea, have been and continue to exert their vital influence in me.

My nannies taught me to sing, and through their singing and speech, I learned to write verses not in an exotic or bizarre form but with a humbleness and affection. I was first an imitator of Pablo Neruda. My voice filled up on his verses as on a feast. One fills oneself until there is not an empty space, until one becomes the voice of the other. We–the young poets of my generation, especially the women poets–did not only want to write like him, but recite like him. It was impossible to escape his voice, his marine zoology. It was nevertheless highly difficult to imitate Neruda's bestiary and incredibly hard to be original in the shadow of this "controlling father."

The other influential figure–influential perhaps only in the case of women–who was a part of our poetic history and of the Latin American imaginary lyricism was the poet Gabriela Mistral, the professor, the rural teacher, the infertile mother. Her voice was calm and never grandiloquent.

Imagine the difficult task of comparing one's reflection to the vision of this rural teacher, the one who spoke to the poor children, to the single women. Was this to be the destiny of female poets? The phenomenon of Mistral, of being catalogued as the saintly teacher, affected the poetic undertakings of Chilean women writers. The figure of Gabriela Mistral and the presence of her humility allowed for a hybrid literary nature. Mistral sings like one obsessed in the silent midst of anonymity in a solitary voice that allows the possibility of a new silence. One no longer sings simply to gain restful sleep but rather to foster life. Gabriela Mistral, like the nannies who make up the lullabies, reawakens folklore but uses it as the best method to bring people together.

Undoubtedly, she was skilled and developed her own self-censorship, using her role as a teacher to legitimize her profession as a poet and her strong artistic vocation. In this way, she managed to speak to women and create an audience for them.

My writing, like that of many other women, has embedded itself in a dislocated axis. On one hand, I say what cannot be said. But I learned to censure myself, to make up excuses, to apologize for what I write and what I should write, for what I am, for my talent, and for being successful, even when all of it is simply the by-product of chance. I find it difficult to legitimize my profession. Not having invented gestures or masks, I write honestly about myself and about others. At times, when I speak about a woman's or a man's body without deceitful cover-ups or euphemism, when I dare to speak on sexual pleasure or on the senses of touch and smell, or when I speak about torture that is always sexual, puritanical critics smile and attempt to pry into my personal life rather than view the text itself and its ramifications as they relate to each reader's conscience.

LEGITIMACY, CONCEALMENT AND TRUTH

The problem of legitimizing what one writes is a constant in my writing. Repeatedly, I am asked why I ally myself to those who are marginal. Is it a tactic to gain fame? Is it to hide arrogance?

Questions about the constant desire to legitimize one's self, to explain one's actions—as Mistral had to explain why she wrote poems about maternity when she never gave birth to a child—continue to circle around me. Gradually, I am approaching the wisdom of the coyote: I no longer excuse myself. I am. I dare. I accept myself.

During the last fifteen years of the Chilean dictatorship, and especially at age seventeen while living in voluntary exile, I lived physically separated from my country. Ironically, although in my heart I always lived in Chile, I was actually born in the United States. But I dreamed about Chile, and every morning, in that austere and remote New England, I would say, "Good morning, Chile."

Exile, the act of seeing without being seen and of seeing everything from an outsider's vantage point, provided me the tools to deepen my commitment to poetry. The position of permanent foreigner allowed me to have a broader vision and to remain alert. The outer margin is a marvelous location.

I arrived in the U.S. with a body of marine poetic images different from those found in this insular, Saxon country. I arrived without knowing the dominant language and quickly learned to hold on to my own, to its incantatory power and nuances, to its subtleties and strength. I still follow fervently the multicolored comings and goings of language.

I continue to live in a hybrid world, in a complex and anomalous bilingual world. But this was also the world of my childhood. I was a bourgeois young girl, privileged and curious, who attended a private school, sharing my afternoons with the maids. I even learned to speak like them. But I was a Jewish girl living in a Catholic country, and the end, I sided with the underprivileged because, as a woman, I was also a stranger in my own country.

My formative experiences as a writer coincided with the rise to power of the military dictatorship in my country, which was when my family immigrated to the United States. The fact that I was an exile lent me a certain degree of legitimacy, both social and political. Distant from political censorship, from repression and torture, I was able to write about the eyes of the dead, of the mutilated bodies, of those who disappeared with no tombstone to mark their burial place. I made this lexicon of horror a part of the daily life of those who are persecuted, and especially, of the women forever ensnared in the veils of terror. From a distance, I could be one of them, and my position as foreigner allowed me to cry out against social indifference.

For years, my poetry has been a literary vehicle for political activism and for promoting women's social revolution. I have spoken of the mothers of Plaza de Mayo, of those women whose intense gaze could almost bring their children back to life, mend the fences. I cannot speak for them; I live in a foreign land, with a language spoken by a privileged people. Still, being always the "other," the one who writes in the margins, allows me to strongly identify with those who live on the outskirts of society. As years went by, this state of ambiguity, this hybrid nature, became the cause for great fear in me. But now I have begun to feel comfortable in this position, in the same way that witches, mad women, and vagabonds might learn to love what they are, to enjoy preparing their brews or wandering endlessly through lands without frontiers or pre-established codes.

My poetry opens a landscape of images, of love scenes captured in intermittently sharp memories, and peers into those areas I have called the "zones of pain." I reinvent myself. Like my literary grandmothers–Gabriela Mistral, Maria Luisa Bombal and Violeta Parra–I also create my space from without. I disfigure myself by looking inward, and I endeavor to create motifs of life in daily rituals. This is how art expands, the way it becomes mutual, powerful and universal.

From my foreignness—an orphanhood of a sort, a chasm–I denounce my country of residence as well as that other land in which, through my dreams, I have taken up residence. This time, nonetheless, I have the advantage and the legitimate right to see them both from afar. I speak about the schism in North American society and of the political violence in Chile from the outside. This allows me the freedom to speak my mind.

Despite my fair skin and deep blue eyes, being a foreigner, though a privileged one, has afforded me the opportunity to form an alliance with the underprivileged. I fully identify with the voiceless people, with the Hispanics in the U.S., with the people of color—since color does not exist deep beneath the skin. "One sees wisely and deeply only when one looks with the heart," as Saint-Exupéry's *Little Prince* so aptly stated.

My work to uphold human rights has turned out to be an immense–if satisfying–ministry, as my poetry has also been. No longer viewing me as the blond girl from some remote corner of the world, Latin American women or "U.S. Hispanic" organizations began to accept me as someone who shared a common language with them. Thus, my active work in poetry and human rights are the most essential aspects of my life's work and of myself. These are inseparable elements, for it would be impossible to live a life as an artist separate from my life as a political entity. Making politics and constructing poems require authenticity and courage. Language gives one away, and faked feelings transform words into lies. I believe in words. I endeavor to have the poem come as close to the truth as possible. As my mentor, I have chosen Clarice Lispector. In her book of voices and deliberations, *The Foreign Legion*, she states:

> The process of writing consists of errors, most of them necessary, of courage and indolence, despair and hope, of growing awareness, of sustained feeling (not thought), which leads nowhere and suddenly what you thought as nothingness turns out to be your own terrifying contact with life. The moment of recognition must be received with the greatest innocence, with the same innocence in which we are born.[2]

Clarice Lispector's words bring me closer to clarity in my writing. I receive this feast of words with humbleness. I am as awestruck before words—and this perpetual awe is the pulse of a disturbing yet wondrous sign—as I am when I listen to women sing out loud or softly.

Poetry, awe, and humbleness are the keys to what I write. They are the elements present in what I tell. I marvel at the possibility of holding a hand, of composing a verse or feeling the intensity of words strike a deep chord within me. I am humbled by the slightest hint of emotion and astonished by the magic force in words that can alter themselves, transforming the text—no longer what it appeared to be, because one word is reborn as another.

MY TEACHERS

I remember and invoke the name of generous and dignified Gabriela Mistral, who liked to write outdoors, notebook resting on her knees, always looking at the sky; or Maria Luisa Bombal who said that the only important thing was to write well and with poetry in the writing. I invoke Violeta Parra who was always turning seventeen to love with all the possibilities open to loving, with all of childhood in a glance.

Violeta Parra was a marginal, indigent woman, selling her paintings on the streets by the riverside. Gabriela Mistral spoke of bare feet, of Indians and of Jews. I am a part of them; I bend to drink the water of heritage that I receive from them. I am a woman, and that is why I approach the children, the poor, the marginal, and the lepers. And one must not forget that I am Jewish and therefore carry within me the history of horror and infamy. My sisters died in concentration camps; they were burned at the stake like the witches of Salem or Medieval times. Just like the mothers of Plaza de Mayo, like the homeless, I am a part of them. I imagine myself in the pyres of death, but I know I am a survivor. I have been saved by poetry, by love, and by that constant awe that comes from writing.

Translated by Monica Bruno

POETRY: AN ACT OF LOVE

I always thought that the peculiar geography of Chile—a land surrounded on one side by snow-covered mountains and on the other by the indomitable spirit of the sea—made it a land of poets. In exile, I came to understand that Chile was also a land of clowns. I discovered this through converations with a young student named Julio. He told me how he had been arrested and then banished to the remote territory of Pisagua—one of the most untamed places in the southern Chilean wilderness—where evenings bring nightmares of the dead. When he told me this, I realized that there is little difference between a clown and a poet. Both are expert at the arts of imagery and brevity, and both struggle to integrate joy and laughter into everyday existence.

There was an abundance of poets and clowns in my country during the fateful years of the Chilean military dictatorship. Despite everything, there was laughter. Words helped us to survive, to create a possible alternative and a new way of telling, doing, and speaking. Laughter also enabled us to cry.

On that ominous day in September 1973, young Chilean citizens, workers, beggars, and pregnant women were taken away to the National Stadium, where thousands of people were summrily tortured and killed. It is said that in the stadium in the evenings poetry was recited and the songs of Violeta Parra were sung. One of the prisoners in that stadium was folk singer and guitarist Victor Jara, who sang even though his hands had been mutilated. Before he was murdered, he recited one last poem, "Viva la Libertad," or "Long live freedom." On those fateful mornings and portentous evenings, poetry was an everyday activity, a noble lady quickened by the breath of life, by circumstance, and by common fear.

Despite censorship and publishing houses that closed their doors in fear, "due to unforeseen circumstances," or because they were ordered to do so, poetry flourished in an unexpected way during those years. It flourished like the everlasting presence in Chile of wildflowers on a rugged trail, the green of open space, and poplar trees with their enormous gray-brown canopies. Young people wrote on newspapers and cardboard boxes. Sometimes they sold their poems on buses or gave them away to those willing to listen to them.

Between the seventies and eighties, an exceptional group of writers was established from all over the country. Motivated by the eye of censorship, they developed a powerful use of language and a vital sense of social awareness. These writers astutely figured out the meanings of the echoes of words, their gentle sounds and cadences. Since gatherings of even three persons were forbidden, as were cemetery visits, poetic activity emerged as a dialogue between two individuals with a desire to listen to each other. Homemakers shared poems and recipes. After work, men read the odes of Neruda. Sometimes they would tuck away the poems which had been given to them on a bus or at a demonstration.

What was most compelling about this phenomenon during the time of the dictatorship was the fact that poetry acquired an unexpected and powerful meaning. It no longer belonged to any cloister, academic institution, or to authoritarian militarism. Poetry was intuitive and spontaneous. People began to claim it as their own. Poetry saved them, helped them meditate, and healed them. It was a prodigious, authentic act.

In those years, many women, relegated to back rooms and to political and official obscurity, had a vision and they became conspicious protagonists. One of the most extraordinary figures of that time was the young artist and cultural activist Pía Barros. Pía states that during the military dictatorship she slept with her clothes on believing that on any frantic evening the police might come for her and take her children away. The night democracy returned to Chile, she put her pajamas on for the first time in seventeen years, and out from under her bed she took the thouands of poems and stories she had been hiding.

Pía Barros created a unique and remarkable art form during the era of the dictatorship, and from cultural artisanry, she engendered an authentic poetic art. Pía invented a new way to create literature using potato sacks. Inside small satchels made from these sacks, she hid short fiction, love stories, and kitchen recipes. On street corners near elegant supermarkets or on the outskirets of Santiago, Pía sold her satchels, and with beautiful and morbid curiosity, women eagerly bought them.

Following this, Pía Barros did other types of work with art objects. *Microcuentos* or "bus stories," were books made in the shape of a small bus. Those stories told of earlier bus rides and reminded us of the dictatorship and of how we no longer dared to look at the sky or whisper to one another.

Poetry spread, but not only through the written word. Chilean *arpilleristas,* or embroiderers, sewed stories of love and loneliness into sackcloth tapestries made from scraps and remnants. They managed to create beautiful objects and to talk about faith and compassion in a voiceless, dehumanized society.

At that time, the use of leftover materials was widespread. To tell stories of fear, for example, Pía Barros used plain wrapping paper and deteriorating old sacks. *Arpilleras,* or sack-cloth tapestries, brought together cloth from used clothing and small fragments of dry branches and leaves. It was as if all nature existed to delight those who recreated life as an expression of beauty from discarded objects. The things of poverty were never the patrimony of dictatorship. What was previously invisible now gave off a new radiance through the prism and gaze of poetry.

Cecilia Vicuña, another poet, titled one of her books *Precario* (Precarious). In it, she spoke about small bits of rubbish on the beach. Through stories and poems, she reconstructed what had been left behind.

Poetry flourished in my country. It wouldn't be held back; no one could contain it. Words had a certain erotic quality to them and played a revitalizing role. During the dictatorship years, people who were "censured" embraced each other. And just as there was an urgent need to touch and to write, there was also an urgency to create and to compose, to recite poetry, and to feel kinship with other people.

At that moment in time, words took on a sacred significance, not in the apostolic sense but in the sense that life itself gains more and more immediacy. Telling was important in order to recover what had not been told and also to eliminate fear. It was important to talk so as not to forget. The dialogues that fostered an exchange of gifts, which were often poems, were also important.

With the advent of democracy, fear came to an end. Poetry, however, continued at a mad pace, versatile and novel. Poetic activity expanded in the form of literary workshops. Beginning in 1989 in democratic Chile, tremendous enthusiam abounded for the workshop phenomenon. Pía Barros was one of the organizers of the first literary workshops in Chile. They functioned on a daily basis, in simple fashion, and in delapitated houses, regardless of the heat or the cold. Pía's workshops were advertised in the newspapers with the idea of bringing together vast numbers of people. In different regions of the country and in Santiago, both rich and poor, on buses or in elegant cars, came to poetry and narrative workshops. The workshops went beyond any conventional meaning of generations, family ties, or established order. Those who participated in these workshops ranged from domestic workers to senators' wives. All were motivated by the frenetic desire to talk, to speak, to tell stories. Poetry previously had flourished in secrecy. Now it was shouting, exclaiming, speaking out loud. And that is precisely what the workshop phenomenon is about: the articulation of the collective word and a search for silenced memories.

Important writers emerged from these workshops, including the young fiction writer Andrea Maturana and Sonia Guralnik, who wrote stories based upon her own experiences in Russia during the pogroms and in Chile during the dictatorship. Creative workshops surfaced in an unprecedented manner for both men and women, young and old. Somehow, they all joined together in a remarkable cultural space within the creative spirit of a nation that did not allow itself to be silenced. That nation chose another language, other ways of speaking. Right now in Chile, citizens are reconstructing all the years that were lived in secrecy. Once again, people greet each other and tell each other about their lives. Once again, people are noisy. Be they ill-tempered or pleasant, they are never silent. Once more, poetry occupies a place at the center of things, the heart of life. Poetry is a queen presiding over a court of rich and poor. She is a loyal friend to the persecuted and the silent, a veritable light shining through seventeen years of darkness.

Translated by Diane Russell-Pineda

HOW TO SPEAK
WITH THE DEAD?

And there they were, numbed in their millennial and captivating pain. They were there, inclined, dangling in an invisible net of suspended time. I approached them. I wanted to speak to them, but what could I ask them? How could I comfort them? By what right could I enter lives sealed by political violence? How to ask them what it means to be the mother of a disappeared? Of a political prisoner? Why should I see them cry?

To be Latin American and of my generation, those born between 1945 and 1955, the so-called generation of "disenchantment," implies being fully conscious of the dictatorships that invaded the Southern Hemisphere in a systematic way for almost twenty years. The role of the writer, which is wholly integrated in the political tasks of these countries, is of extreme importance and complexity. What does a dictatorship signify and how does one document it? Up to what point is it feasible to make poetry about the tortured body? Who can say it is authentic for a writer to be responsible for the political violence of a country?

These questions are necessary and serve as continuous guidelines for those of us who write about the polemic of state terrorism, about its victims and its survivors. Throughout Latin America's literary history there has been a powerful alliance between the tasks of the writer and her political role. Beginning with the organization of the Latin American republics of the nineteenth century when the concepts of nation, modernity, and culture were established, politics and government became interchangeable concepts in society. Both the political identity and the artistic identity were established as true occupations of politicians, thus converting the men and women of letters into public figures. Such were the cases of José Marti in Cuba, Che Guevara in Bolivia, Romulo Gallegos, president of Venezuela, and Pablo Neruda, candidate to the presidency of Chile during the government of Salvador Allende.

For José Miguel Oviedo, twentieth century Latin American literature was born at a time in which it was impossible to renounce its vocational link to the problems of creating a conscience. These writers belonged to an elite, they had privileges and access to culture. Therefore, they assumed the voice of the underprivileged as a function of the intellectual's solidarity with the people. In the field of poetry, says Oviedo, this phenomenon continued to develop into a deeper form. The American preoccupation with the indigenous people and with the marginal, as well as the nineteenth century influence and the pervasive romanticism, make Latin American poetry a hybrid genre born under the seal of social protest.

During the twentieth century, the quintessential problem regarding the role of the writer in society has been difficult to articulate. The old polemic surrounding the commitment of a writer surfaced again with renewed intensity during the 1970s. The poets of this decade recreated the spirits of Pablo Neruda and Cesar Vallejo, who during the Spanish Civil War created two of the most important texts of political Latin American poetry: *Spain, Keep this Chalice Away from Me* (1932) by Vallejo and *Spain in the Heart* (1930) by Neruda. Neruda explained that during that period he could not see the stars, the plains, or the beloved corn. Nevertheless, he says:

> I have managed to touch the naked heart of my people and to realize with pride that in this heart lies a secret which is stronger than the springtime, more fertile and resounding than the oats and the water, the secret of the truth, which my humble, solitary, and forsaken people gather from the dregs of their hard land and raise high in their triumph, so that all the people of the world may consider it, respect it and imitate it.

The sense of responsibility and of peace is one of the central banners that define the Latin American poetry of the period. In Cuba, in 1949, Nicolás Guillén continued this trend by writing about the social indignation caused by the neocolonialism of the Caribbean. In his well-known poem "West Indies Ltd.," where Guillén encompasses the topics of dependence and colonialism, there are echoes of Neruda and Vallejo. Beginning in the 1950s, Latin American poetry dominated the national culture more than prose, a phenomenon that inverted itself in the 1990s. Paradoxically, the Latin American intellectual believed that revolution could be created with books and that the public had to be responsible for the problems of society and should understand the privileged author who spoke for the voiceless. But who, in this illiterate continent, is the audience for authors whose books have limited circulation and may be known to the people of the big cities but remain completely unknown to the inhabitants of rural areas?

After the Cuban revolution of the 1960s and the presence of the many dictatorships in the Southern Cone, there was a different scope in Latin America's cultural process. The proliferation of the capitalistic system, where it was almost impossible to maintain a utopian ideology, caused the literature of commitment of the 1960s to slowly decline. The Cuban Revolution became progressively more anguishing, and the Latin American intellectual began to emerge with a new conscience around the identity of literature and its duties as a citizen.

Repressive dictatorships drastically transformed the course of Latin American literature in the 1970s. Censure, saying what cannot be said, caution and silence all became new ways of expressing one's self. But perhaps it is during this period that the issues of literature and its commitment and literature within the political context emerged once again.

The 1970s brought scenes of lacerated bodies, of bookburning, of the military, and of the clashes at the universities. The human rights movement emerged with great strength. Many women began to speak the language of men, that is, the language of politics and of the streets. However, the vision, the specter of violence remained as an unspeakable entity. How does one speak of clandestine prisons? How does one speak of Jews tortured in the basements of homes in Buenos Aires next to photographs of Hitler and Mussolini?

More than ever, the Latin American writers were flooded with different codes and messages. What to say when one cannot say anything? What is the use of writing poetry during a period of unrestrained fascism? A time when books do not circulate? Where poetry proliferates in the prisons? How to rescue and validate memory?

The debate is accentuated when the Latin American writer goes into exile and recovers memory and nostalgia through the temporary and borrowed scenery of an imaginary landscape. The artist remains, codifies language, and molds writing in order to join the spheres of literature and social commitment. The dilemma of the writer's commitment intensifies even more. For Benedetti, an exiled Uruguayan writer, literature must be communal and jointly binding, in the service of every position taken by the revolutionary left. On the other extreme is Mario Vargas Llosa, whose primary obligation is, first and foremost, to the Creator. I believe that between Vargas Llosa and Garcia Marquez a great fusion and tension is produced in Latin American literature. Many writers in exile also felt preoccupied by the exaggerated militarism and by a literature that served the state.

However, the problems around this ideology become almost inconsequential if we begin to outline the paradoxical debate around the systems of representation—the horror and the problems which held great similarity with those of the Holocaust and its literature.

Political repression led the Latin American writer to outline her praxis, not based on the concept of nation and culture, but rather around the impossibility of representing with an aesthetic symbolic discourse the horror of the political discourse. How does one speak of the victims and the victimizers? Is it possible to establish a poetic discourse about torture? The problem of writing and acting around the issues of literature and violence implies opening old wounds and questioning the limits of the repression. It also implies the author's participation in a moral and religious discourse where the nation and ideology do not appear in abstract form, but rather, where the life of the individual is being questioned.

The inability to represent pain is manifested in various forms. In Chile, the majority of writers that speak in a conjectural way about the political repression are part of the generation that disappeared. They write as survivors. There is in them the inviolable transference and that sense of atavistic destiny that implies a privileged zone, responsibility and guilt. Memory and its lacunae in these texts function and identify themselves with history. They represent history and are part of it.

An interesting phenomenon occured: Chilean woman writer Diamela Eltit who, with her strange and overpowering novel or fragment entitled *Lumperica* took us to the core of fear and its representation. The novel takes place in a plaza abandoned during curfew. The female protagonist is the only one who inhabits the city, a city of the dead, of the disappeared. This text creates an impact because the language Eltit uses brings us closer to the language of emptiness.

Also of interest is a novel written by the North American writer Lawrence Thorton, *Imagining Argentina*. This novel is also populated by spaces filled with fear and pain and the dreaded Ford Falcons that roam the city, which is empty save for the captors who dedicate themselves to arbitrarily collecting plundered bodies. However, this novel does not fully convince us. It is too detective-like. The fiction is too pure and, therefore, distances us from history, and a landscape covered with palm trees in the Southern Cone is a contradiction. It seems as if we were reading a text about magic, not about horror. This is not harsh criticism, but it would be worth it to ask ourselves: Why, out of two texts on the same topic, does one have a greater impact on us than the other? Is this a problem related to vision, wisdom, historical precision, or a new approach to truth? Would it be related to the issue of how to present history as fiction, how to conceptualize horror, how to represent mutilated bodies?

These questions are the ones confronted by the writers of my generation, the "disenchanted" generation. We are and are not the disappeared. We *could* have been disappeared, but we survived. How do we speak of the identity of the survivors?

In my country, many authors opted for one of two paths: silence, which signaled a posture in the world and a way to frame memory, or the voice which moved literature to the scenario of forbidden places and of the marginal. For example, Diamela Eltit read in a whorehouse and lacerated her body in homage to and alliance with the tortured.

Strangely enough, literature allowed us an ambiguous distancing. Literature, unlike the evening news, did not make us believe that we lived in the midst of horror, which is why there was a boom of literary texts about political repression. We were besieged by it because it was easier to read, and paradoxically, seemed less real.

My experiences in exile helped me understand the periphery, to look at my country from the sphere of a foreigner. My first literary works were about women who made *arpilleras,* tapestries with political focus. In them, torture and repression are present in their full and desolate nudity but, at the same time, camouflaged. In the midst of death, children floated on a river. Or was it corpses? The experience of working with the *arpilleras* brought me closer to literature. The words were embroidered. The text was measured and sewn. The *arpilleras* said what one could not say, and they represented it in seemingly naive drawings, as if the cloth were an escape in the face of so much horror.

Little by little I got used to talking about the disappeared, the political prisoners, and the jailers. To speak of them, to approach the vocabulary of the torn, of the unusual, of the ominous, became part of my everyday language. For years the presence of the disappeared inhabited my waking and sleeping hours until I was finally able to speak like them. I lost the feeling of objectivity. I did not see them as beings occupying the uninhabited spaces of absence. In some way, they were everywhere. To speak of them did not become a way of reconceptualizing the horror, but neither was it a form of creating fiction from history. The transfer was complete. Poetic language was also part of this experience. That is why I could speak of blindfolds, thin wall partitions, and grills; I became familiar with the lexicon of terror.

My job, that of recording history, of witnessing, of telling, and of rescuing memory became a vocation and an obsession. Aesthetics no longer held center stage for me and it became more vital to simply make literature. Like Carlos Fuentes would say, I was creating fast literature, useful and necessary, just some "emergency letters."

An essential change took place the day I finished my interviews with a group of detained-disappeared in Chile, in 1983. It was a misty afternoon, like most afternoons in Santiago, and a group of women approached me holding little photographs, tokens, and clothes belonging to their children. They were gifts for me from ghosts outside of time and space. I felt my body covered with wounds, and knew that my challenge was to make the dead speak, not to elaborate on empty space, on the absence of the disappeared.

My poetry underwent a radical change. In the book *Zones of Pain,* I transferred the image from that misty afternoon. The poems were the images of those women, makers and searchers. Poetry could not fully recreate their experiences, but it had the power of making them universal. The images transcended the logic of space and language. The images of the clandestine prisons went beyond the country's borders. They went to other dimensions, they reached the woods made of wires. Now I ask myself what right I had to speak of them. Why did I appropriate their zones and the theme of pain? What model did I follow to speak about the dead?

I must say that in my poetry I chose to use their language. My texts are full of images that sprang from the conversations that I had with these women. The images of bodies in pain, of the cold and the dark are common in my poetry. I reproduced the language of the mothers, a language highly aesthetic and metaphorical. I heard their language and I wrote it in a different format: poetry.

Adorno said that after Auschwitz there could be no poetry. I believe that poetry, with its atemporal qualities, its symbolic language that identifies yet at the same time negates, allows me to create a zone of ambivalence. It allowed me to speak of these women because the poet speaks from the area of identity, from the sphere of the "I."

The boldness and nudity of the poems allowed me to create in the text a scenario of the history without history. In opposition to narrative, which speaks of history as fiction, poetry allows history to take root in itself.

My experiences with the imaginary in poetry were more fruitful than when I began to write about the mother of three disappeared. Prior to that, my political work took place under the sign and identity of a group that allowed for a jointly binding alliance, allowed the voices to be confused and gave no autonomy to the poet.

In 1989, when my son was almost a year old, I went to Buenos Aires, Argentina to work with one of the founders of the Mothers of the Plaza de Mayo. I wanted to write a book about this woman's relation to the movement she helped establish. Through the language of documenting history, through the interviews, I learned to respect the cadences and the zones of silence. To work with an individual is much more complex than to speak with women about a communal experience. I made mistakes. I thought an individual could be a metaphor for a group. I forgot that I was speaking to an individual person, that there existed the element of the ego, of silence and self-censure that did not allow me to reach the history or the fiction.

I had various possibilities: I could write history under a political discourse, mask the poetry, invent and create a myth about the person I was interviewing. Maybe, though, I committed the grave mistake of reappropriating the political and social symbolism. I believed that in my art there was a radical intervention between her reality and mine. When writing poetry about political discourse, none of the questions I mentioned earlier invaded me. I did not even think that I was appropriating someone else's pain. I believed poetry carried within it the zones of silence and all possible representations.

My attempt at reproducing the pain of a woman whose three children had been disappeared by the State became an impossibility. Her silences did not relate the horror she had undergone, nor did they help me sense what she was going to say. On the contrary, those uncomfortable and acute silences helped me understand that I could not write about this woman with the language of history. I then asked myself: Would it be possible to reproduce history as part of everyday life? I could not do that either, and my text became a series of fragments to be continued, to be organized. After repeated frustrating interruptions in the interview process, I returned to poetry. I approached her with respect, knew that I could only write about René Eppelbaum with an aesthetic imagery that would not represent her in her own historical dimension. I would write about an individual who did not want to be history, but nevertheless was history.

My book was not a standard text about the "dirty war" in Argentina, nor was it a collection of collages. I wrote about my experience with René Eppelbaum as a fragmented discourse. I situated her in Plaza de Mayo, kerchief on her head, or at home, naked and alone. I spoke of the altars that inhabit her home; I said she was fat and alone. My truth translated into personal offense, but I transformed the political image and made her a martyr, a victim, a human being.

Regardless of the relevance of this topic, *Mothers of the Plaza de Mayo: the Story of René Epelbaum 1976-87* has gone completely unnoticed, unlike my other two books of poetry. The protagonist of the text does not want to see herself in it. She feels I stripped her of virtue. In making her human, I took away the Plaza and left her alone with her dead. Now I approach that text and I see that it is a fragmented and interrupted poetic discourse, the life of a truncated being with conversations and pauses. I presented her as vulnerable and alone. She told me she had not said such a thing, and I answered that she had not said anything at all. I could not inscribe her in the language of history, so I made her poetry and fragment.

The text edited by Professor Saul Friedlander, *Probing the Limits of Representation: Nazism and the "Final Solution,"* presents complex questions. In light of the Holocaust, it has been proven that it is almost impossible to make people talk about the inexplicability of genocide, even though the images, the photographs of the concentration camps, like the photos of the Mothers of Plaza de Mayo, go beyond spoken and written discourse.

In my experience, I could only formulate questions without answers. Is there a coherent self that can write and speak of political repression? Or does the being that writes, due to the nature of the topic, remain a fragment, distanced from the course of history? Is it possible for the literature of political violence to defy the political conscience of the society that allows violence? How do you avoid the creation of a myth around the individual without offending? What is the correct distance between the victims and those who write about them? How does one speak of fear? How do you speak as a testimonial writer without ever having been imprisoned?

This last question seems to be of particular interest because it deals with the ways of appropriating certain discourses and modalities of being. To me the most powerful text on the political repression in Argentina is the book by Jacobo Timmerman because he says he writes as a witness and that puts us closer to history. Timmerman, in his book *Prisoner Without a Name–Cell Without a Number*, constantly alludes to the pogroms and the history of the Holocaust that supposedly would have prepared him for the Argentinean holocaust. However, Timmerman says:

> So many battles, so many tortures, so many blows, it was logical to assume that I thought I knew everything about being a political prisoner, how one suffered in prison, how a tortured man felt. Well, I did not know anything and it is impossible to convey what I now know...

> What does the human being feel? The only thing I can think of is this: they were ripping off my flesh. But it wasn't the flesh. Yes, I

know. They didn't even leave scars. But I felt that they were rip-ping off my flesh. But, what else? I cannot think of anything else. Any other sensation? Not at the moment. But were they hitting you? Yes, but it did not hurt.

Basically, the book by Timmerman indicates that one cannot communicate the magnitude of the pain. He who has not been tortured cannot understand or recognize the magnitude of the inexplicable. Along with Timmerman's assertions, it would be useful to mention David Caroll's position:

We are required to judge the philosophical, literary, political, his-torical, and moral effect of the different ways of talking or not talk-ing or not talking about "that" (the Shoah) and yet we do not have the systems of belief or knowledge, the rules, the historical certainty or the philosophical or political concepts necessary to derive or determine judgment...This does not diminish the role of the critical faculty but on the contrary makes it all the more crucial and neces-sary.

What are the formulas and poetic licenses, the narrative strategies to speak of collective extermination? How does one establish a dialogue with the audi-ence? How to manipulate them or not manipulate them? Maybe it would be enough to defy fiction and history by speaking about torture. In my experi-ence, portraying the pain of the disappeared, of the tortured body, fluctuates under two coordinates: that of an internal distancing and that of poetic lan-guage which, in the end, is devoid of realism but goes beyond reality. My book *Circles of Madness* contains photographs of the mothers. The text uses the trick of speaking about the photographs. It is in those images that I find my identity, and I allow myself to hide behind them. Another interesting aspect is that the photographs allow me to place myself within a symbolic geography, a historical period. Paradoxically, history and its absence are the strategies used to speak about the unspeakable, to appropriate the history of madness without pretending to clarify things, but somehow salvaging memo-ry, reflecting upon it and constantly questioning it.

I believe it is good advice. Once it has been decided that human beings can be tortured, there is nothing that can stop it. And it is better to calmly allow one's self to be led toward pain and by pain, than to fight as if one were a normal human being: the vegetative attitude can save one's life.

"In that solitary universe of the tortured, all attempts to relate to reality were a painful effort that led me to nothing."

Translated by Monica Bruno

SO WE WILL NOT FORGET:
LITERATURE AND HUMAN RIGHTS
IN LATIN AMERICA

In Greek mythology, the beautiful Philomela was raped by her brother-in-law, who cut out her tongue so that she could not tell what he had done. Philomela wove the story of her tragedy into a tapestry for her sister so neither would forget it. This myth currently holds special power to those living under the authoritarian governments to Latin America.[1] During the 1960s and 1970s, many Latin American families were decimated by violent governments: repression, torture, and rape were common occurrences. Thousands of others were forced to leave and experience the hardships of exile under foreign skies.

Those who remained faced questions of how to survive in a country where truth was gagged and of how to invent a mode of writing that could reach a reader who was suffering and in distress. In the presence of these questions, the risk to the writer as well as to the reader became a metaphor for the repression and terror imposed by fascist governments. For example, the public book burnings in Santiago in 1973 also represented the burning of possible readers.

A pervasive pattern found in these right and left-wing authoritarian Latin American dictatorships is the political compromise of the Latin American intellectual. The Argentine author Julio Cortazar affirmed that writing has ceased to have a game-like function among us and that "to write and to read is increasingly a possibility of acting extraliterarily, although many of our most significant books do not contain explicit messages nor do they seek ideological or political converts. To write and read is a form of action."[2]

The Latin American writer of the 1970s, like the journalist, cinematographer, and photographer, is the one who prevents the truth from disappearing, the one who searches for the testimony of eyewitnesses, of the forgotten ones, offering a taste of life and validity to the word. Written literature, oral testimonies, and public performances on forbidden streets demonstrate that Latin America hums with life despite the collective massacres, book burnings, and obligatory silence.

The theme of human rights is intrinsically linked to a literature that does not forget and that refuses to be silenced. In this way, these writers become the survivors, the living voices, the witnesses who defy censorship, self-censorship, and, at times, death. I have chosen to focus on prose because of its greater density of social and historical material. Nevertheless, poetry offers a field of study of equal richness.[3]

THE RELATIONSHIP BETWEEN

THE TORTURER AND THE TORTURED AS A LITERARY DEVICE

The broken and mutilated body recurs in the works of many authors, especially in that of two writers of particular interest: Mario Benedetti and Elvira Orphee. Mario Benedetti, the prolific Uruguayan writer who spent many years in exile in Cuba, introduces the almost symbiotic relationship that exists between torturer and tortured, between executioner and victim. His novel, *Pedro y el capitan* (Pedro and the Captain) is unforgettable and revealing: The confrontation between the torturer and the tortured is not presented as the meeting of two monsters but of two human beings, both victims of the same repressive system.

When the torturer talks about his children, family, and mundane life after the "electric sessions," the reader-accomplice, observing this dialogue, in turn interrogates him or herself or imagines the life of a torturer at the end of the workday. This situation compels the reader to think about the torturers in present day Latin America who have been forgiven by governments for their crimes. When Pedro, the torture victim, asks the anonymous and hooded torturer about his family, he responds:

Before, you asked me about my family. Yes. I have a wife and a little house. A seven year-old boy and five year-old girl. It is true that it is sometimes hard to face them when I get home from work. I don't torture here, but I hear too many moans, blood-curdling screams, howls of desperation. At times, I arrive with my nerves shot. My hands shake. I'm not very good at this work, but I'm trapped. And so I find a justification for my work: Make the prisoner speak![4]

The uselessness of torture is also portrayed in the silence of the prisoner. Pedro does not speak: he refuses to confess, to denounce his friends, and torture is no more than a futile act of self-indulgence from the point of view of the torturer.

The gag and the blindfold are the usual graphic images of repression in this literature. In *Pedro y el capitan* the victim refuses to speak with a person wearing a hood; he refuses to confess to a man who, by covering his face, is also, to a certain degree, gagged. Pedro's response to the fact that the torturer covers his face is: "No, I don't like it. But it doesn't matter to me. I also want to tell him that, because of the hood, I didn't open my mouth because there is a minimum amount of dignity I must maintain, and a hood is something contemptible."[5]

The act of confession never takes place in this brief but intense text written in the form of a dramatic dialogue. Pedro uses his own silence and the silence of a collective dignity as his only weapon to disarm the torturer: "You offer me the option to live like a dead person and, given this, I prefer to die like a living one."[6]

In *Pedro y el capitan*, as in so many of the literary, as opposed to technical, texts on human rights, we observe both the most and the least noble aspects of the human spirit. In the dialogue between Pedro and the capitan, the torturer ends up being a victim of an unhealthy and surreal situation. The victim, a man who prefers death to treachery, becomes a martyr of political and social conscience.

Pedro y el capitan, originally published in Spain, was banned in its country of origin. For many Latin American intellectuals, the "mother country" has been a haven of political freedom, as Latin America was a refuge for Spaniards during the Spanish Civil War.

Elvira Orphee, an Argentine, is one of the first Latin American women writers to write from the point of view of a torturer. She does this in her novel, *The Angel's Last Conquest,* which, like Beneditti's novel was originally banned in the author's homeland.[7] It was published in Venezuela, and only recently was allowed to enter its country of origin. *The Angel's Last Conquest* exercises a strong hypnotic power over its readers as the author fades into the background and her characters begin to speak for themselves, discussing torture with an objective, technical language, sinisterly precise in its descriptions. The banality of evil and its widespread infusion into society frightens the reader as he or she is made aware of the varying degrees of torture techniques that can be used to punish subversive acts, in many circumstances and in diverse institutions, such as the military academies. The novel leaves the reader without any doubt that torture is the state's main method for maintaining order.

The story told by the torturer reveals his dedication to a mission that must be carried out and his profound sense of duty to the homeland. The narrator must pass through his own process of initiation so as not to identify with the victim. In the chapter titled "Ceremony," an ordered and perfect ritual is performed by the torturer: "Each step must be followed, each rule obeyed, each gesture known in advance."[8]

The body in pain as property of the state is one of the central symbols of this brief and extremely poignant narrative. The separation between the torturer as a unit of the state and the victim as property forces the reader to question the surreal nature of the torturer's life, especially the torturer's fondness for remembering the torturing process' initiation rites with a horrific nostalgia.[9]

The acts of torture and the silenced, blindfolded, and gagged body are used by Orphee and Benedetti in trying to capture the intrinsic relationships between human beings of different political beliefs. Orphee uses the technique of distancing as the only possible way to recreate the act of torture, as a ritual of technical and scientific precision. Benedetti uses an opposite technique: he tries to create an almost friendly relationship where social rigidity disappears and the protagonists must meet and deal with each other on a human level.

When a woman is tortured, it is important to remember that her degradation is double: she is degraded as a political prisoner and as a woman. The Chilean scholar Ximena Bunster affirms that a tortured woman, who can be a mother and therefore of use to the patriarchal system, is transformed into a prostitute, a betrayal of her biological role.[10] Interestingly, we do not find texts where a woman is a torturer, just the constant allusion to women as victims.

Requiem for a Woman's Soul by Omar Rivabella and *Coral de guerra* (War Chorale) by Fernando Alegría deal with the theme of the raped and tortured woman.[11] Rivabella's text is about the protagonist's terror while being gang-raped by a group of officers. Full of technicalities and lacking in depth, it reads more like a manual of physical degradation than a literary work. Basically, the text narrates the story of a priest in a small Argentine city who finds in the trash the diary of a woman who was tortured. The reader slowly enters a world shaped by horror, violence, mutilation, and the sadism of the torturers. Nevertheless, the text focuses more on the explicit confessions of a torture victim than on the human complexities found in the parallel between the torturer and victim.

Coral de guerra presents the metaphor of dictatorship through an assaulted body: the woman who is punished for refusing to confess. The novel's plot involves the love of an officer for his victim, a love established before the military coup in Chile. The officer's unrequited love can be translated into a reading linked to the verifiable historical moment: the relationship between the dictatorship, the officer, and Chile, the tortured woman. Because she refuses to speak and remains silent, the woman is punished for not cooperating with those who exercise the dominant power.

The most prominent voices in the novel are those of the officer, who gives his version of the events in a monologue to the woman's husband, and the missing woman, who tells her own story. She denounces her treatment clearly to the reader and to the aggressor, who does not want to hear them. The relation of power in this novel is clearly understood in the contrast between the naked woman and the officer with all his accoutrement: sword, boots, and belt. The discourse on sexual power in the text is a metaphor for the control that the dictatorship maintains over the country.

In an inner monologue, the anonymous victim understands why the officer subjects her to fear, humiliation, and embarrassment: "He wanted to defeat me through hunger but not to defeat myself or anyone. He tried to change the world with a magic act, and I wanted people to make love in the odor of closed rooms, hugging their cattle prods, crying from happiness or remorse, kissing their swords to believe firmly in their powers."[12]

The officer accuses, punishes, and avenges himself through the rape and kidnapping of the victim, who refuses to denounce or speak, as the victims in the previous texts refused to speak. The victim chooses not to talk as a way of demonstrating her resistance through silence. Not speaking is understood by the officer as a crime that defies his power. The self-imposed silence is a triumph for the victim and, in her silence, the undefeatable resistance of the victim is profiled and established.

Coral de guerra can be read as a text of voices where statements, documents, and memories take on meaning according to the character who articulates the message. In this way, the torturer, the hostage, and the hostage's husband (who only appears at the end of the text) are described with magnificent psychological knowledge of the inner being confronting the power and violation of his or her own body.

The permanent confusion of voices, and the confusion concerning the truth of the narrative fact is an effective device used by the author to dissemble and reconstruct a story where torturer and victim are united in a fluctuation of circumstances. Thus, language itself becomes a boundary between the subjective reality, in this case, the officer's beliefs, and the objective history of Chile during and after the coup d'etat. The text closes with all the voices united in one "I" who speaks with the voice of the officer and reflects on how social and historical processes help to transform the individual:

> Some day, a woman will appear at your house. The same leather jacket, the same blue shorts and sandals. A young girl but be careful; she won't be a child. You will notice it in her eyes, or better, around her eyes. You will see a slight fatigue that isn't really fatigue but knowledge, because she learned a lot with us, and you will notice in her mouth the years she lived during that year.[13]

THE DISAPPEARED-REAPPEARED AND THE NEGATION OF OBLIVION

Disappearances have become perhaps the most diabolical and efficient manifestations of authoritarian regimes in Latin America. At night, friends and relatives await the return home of loved ones, but they do not appear. "Where are they?" becomes the obsessive question of family members who, defying silence, dedicate themselves to continual searches for loved ones who are seldom found. This Machiavellian practice of making people disappear is, at the same time, an act of cowardice. If there are no bodies or traces of these bodies, the totalitarian governments can deny the existence of their victims

The general public still does not fully know the extent of the disappearances, and, for many years, terrified family members were forced to keep quiet. The following represents a legal perspective on disappearances: "Several fundamental rights are violated: the right to freedom, the right to physical integrity and usually the right to life. Disappearance violates the right of legal defense since no warrant for arrest is issued, there is no trial and no public announcement."[14]

Many writers and journalists have publicly denounced the disappearances. There are two basic texts on the disappeared: *Preso sin nombre—celda sin numero* (Prisoner without a name—Cell Without a Number) by Jacobo Timmerman and *The Little School* by Alicia Partnoy.[15] These accounts reveal the anguish and desperate terror experienced by victims imprisoned in clandestine jails but, even more, the works reveal the victims' passion for life and survival.

The case of Jacobo Timmerman is well known. Argentine journalist, defender of human rights, and advocate of nonviolence, Timmerman was arrested in 1976, tortured, and kept imprisoned until he was released in September 1979, thanks to an international outcry. It is important to remember that Timmerman was saved primarily because he was a public figure. How many others have perished as a result of the terrible prods of the electric shock machine in Argentine concentration camps, so similar to those in Hitler's Germany?

To read Timmerman's book is to be blessed by the profound human reflections of a man who was tortured and now bears lucid witness to his own story. Timmerman does not document each moment of his captivity in detail, his brutal treatment, or the humiliations he suffered for being Jewish. Instead, he presents the situation of a wounded man who managed to endure torture, not through the painful memory of his loved ones but through his own passive resistance and ability to empty his mind to survive subhuman conditions.

Timmerman's description of observing another prisoner through a tiny crack in the wall is both chilling and beautiful:

And so I have to talk about you of that long night we spent togeth-
er in which you were my brother, my father, my son, my friend. Or
were you a woman? Then we spent the night as lovers. You were
an eye but you remember that night, don't you? They told me that
you died, that you had a weak heart and couldn't endure the
machine, but they didn't tell me if you were a man or a woman
and, anyway, how could you have died if we defeated death that
night?[16]

The lyricism of this book penetrates the reader's eyes and skin. The most
dominant questions that it poses are: How does a tortured person feel pain?
How does a blindfolded prisoner see light? Timmerman enables us to share
his experience, as far as that is possible:

During the long months of imprisonment, I thought many times
about how I would be able to convey the pain that a tortured per-
son feels, and I always concluded that it was impossible. It is a
pain that does not have a point of reference, revealing symbols or
codes that could serve as a beginning. A human being is taken so
rapidly from one world to another that he/she does not have a way
to find any remaining energy to confront that untethered vio-
lence.[17]

Timmerman, through flashbacks, tells of events that are both grotesque and
surreal in their wickedness. For example, prior to a family being torturedto-
gether, the man's children and wife must feed the him so he can better with-
stand the torture sessions.

The eye, the look that sees despite the blindfold, is Timmerman's illuminat-
ed vision, the vision of a prisoner who defies death and says "yes" to life. His
text is full of visions that will forever resurface in the reader's mind, but that
cannot really be shared or understood by others. Nevertheless, the victim will
always have them: "I believe that the visions through which I entered
Argentina's clandestine prisons and that I have kept with me one by one were
the climactic point, the purest moment of my tragedy. They are here with me.

And although I might want to do it, I couldn't, wouldn't know how to share them with you."[18]

Alicia Partnoy also belonged to the ranks of the disappeared: she was one of approximately 30,000 individuals swallowed up by this new technique of terror. Partnoy, who, along with her young daughter, was, by random luck, released is one of the few women who has converted her pain into a story to be told and not forgotten. Partnoy's book is not a conventional narrative, but is composed of fragments of poetic prose that tell what it is like to live in a cell with your eyes blindfolded. *The Little School*, a name given to one of the concentration camps on the outskirts of Buenos Aires, describes in detail a life that was completely violated.

In the first fragment of the text, "The One Flower Slippers," the protagonist recounts how she was arrested while wearing her husband's slippers, after having slept in her clothes for many months knowing that they would come for her. An instance of tenderness is found in the section entitled "Birthday," where the guards allow the prisoner to have a soda on her birthday.

The senses, the taste of rain, the smell of bread, the sun, things we so often take for granted, take on a shameless lyricism, a humanity that the reader discovers along with Partnoy in this marvelous book of pain and hope. This is shown in the fragment, "Conversation Under the Rain": "This day had been different: The rain had made it different. Shortly after it had begun to rain the smell of damp earth made her come to grips with the fact that she was still alive. She inhaled deeply and a rare memory of freedom tickled her cheekbones."[19]

Another enlightening book about the "disappeared" is Marta Traba's *Conversacion al sur*.[20] The novel is fictitious, but in Latin America today it is difficult to distinguish fiction from reality. Traba's book alludes to this phenomenon. *Conversacion al sur*, translated into English under the title *Mothers and Shadows*, takes place in an atmosphere occupied by victims who roam through the cities, phantoms in countries populated by memories of the missing. Those who survive must learn to exist among the torturers and the tortured.

Mothers and Shadows is a dialogue between two women of different generations sharing memories of what the political repression in three countries of the Southern Cone has cost them. One recalls her lost son, missing in Chile since the beginning of the military coup in 1973. The other remembers her period of political activism in Buenos Aires, her subsequent imprisonment and the loss of her child while she was in jail, and the death of her husband.

The power of the novel lies in its revelation of the total usurpation of one's personal life by the dictatorship in an atmosphere of asphyxia and terror. The individual exists or ceases to exist according to the whim of the state. Given this, the relentless question becomes how to survive the menace one more day. For the protagonists, as well as for readers immersed in this intimate conversation about the Southern Cone, the world is constricted, because under a dictatorship one must live every day facing menace, pain, and, too often, death.

The female protagonists of *Mothers and Shadows* share a world of terror as well as the need to create; they are not content to be mere witnesses of a passing world. Says one:

> "Ah. The brief time we spent together isn't important. The intensity is what counts. The world we glimpsed, the fear we shared. And I don't mind telling you that my hands are perpetually frozen and that they'd gladly reach out to you for warmth. Let's take things one at a time sister. Let's see if we create or are merely witnesses."[21]

EVERYONE'S SONG IS MY OWN SONG: LITERATURE AND TESTIMONY

Testimonial literature is by no means a new literary genre. It dates from the age-old oral tradition where the act of recounting and singing is an essential element. Nevertheless, what is new and a phenomenon of recent years is the fact that these testimonial narratives now appear with greater frequency. Witnesses have always existed, but now, for the first time, the necessary audience and means of communication exist also.[22]

In most of the testimonies available today and systematically published in various parts of the world, what stands out is the tone of pain and terror and the brutality toward the human body. The testimony is a form of struggle where images of impotence and aggression are transformed into a spur to the survivor's memory:

Testimonial literature possesses an incipient historical materialism present in all testimony without artifice, without false narrative voices, since the one who gives the testimony is the narrator. Different from novels, whose form usually implies the outcome, an end that, in certain cases, is only valid as a provisional cancellation of the world and the feeling of otherness that the reading actualizes, the testimonies in their most basic meaning are evidence of a story that continues and a way of living the present.[23]

In Latin America, the testimonial genre is practiced by many writers who lend their voices to the voiceless. Elena Poniatowska in Mexico stands out, having authored such works as *La noche de Tlatelolco,*[24] which tells the story of the 1968 Mexico City massacre of students by the police on the Plaza de Tlateloloco. Also, there is a proliferation of testimonies from people one seldom hears about: farmers from isolated regions, seamstresses, and domestic servants.

It is impossible to enumerate the long list of testimonial books, which range from interviews, as in Patricia Verdugo's *Miedo en Chile*[25] (Fear in Chile) to the narratives of political prisoners in clandestine jails. Books that have received widespread international distribution and that I believe are fundamental within the gamut of testimonial literature include two Cuban books, *Against All Hope: The Prison Memories of Armando Valladares* by Armando Valladares, and *Twenty Years and Forty Days: Life in a Cuban Prison* by Jorge Valls.[26] *Against All Hope* tells the story of Vallandares' twenty years in captivity, from his detention in his own home to his release and escape to Paris where his wife, Martha, was waiting for him. Martha was an ardent, tireless supporter and the one most responsible for his final release. Although the book is not very well written, it is an important testimony about twenty years in a Cuban jail and it exemplifies how totalitarian governments from the right or left employ the same means of control when dealing with political prisoners.

Jorge Valls' book is a much more passionate account that has not received the recognition it deserves. Valls, a leading activist in the University of Havana's student movement, fought during the Cuban Revolution and was imprisoned for twenty years until his release in 1985. Valls' narrative is a powerful and compelling saga of one man's life in prison. He also describes his "trial," during which he was denied access to a lawyer and was not allowed to present witnesses in his defense.

This memoir is a testimony to the strength, dignity, and triumph of the human spirit. It shows us a man who was able to survive without hatred or resentment toward those who imprisoned him. On the contrary, Valls' profound feeling of solidarity with humanity was intensified by his prison experience:

> In jail a unique human link is forged. No one has ever seen us so humiliated and powerless, not even our parents, but no one has an equal power to comfort us with a word, an attitude, or a mere physical presence. No one has ever been more closely bound than two convicts. 27

Unlike testimonial literature that stresses only the ideological issues of imprisonment, this narrative is an almost lyrical account of one prisoner's adversities and survival. The book speaks naturally of life in isolation and of psychological and physical torture, but it is not intended as a shocking expose of the Cuban government. It remains the story of a man deeply committed to his people and, of course, to his beloved country. The powerful voice of Jorge Valls, a renowned poet and winner of many international prizes, draws us into the nightmarish life of a political prisoner with its terror, anguish, and fear. We feel what it is like to be a helpless victim. But above all, Valls' liberation teaches that freedom, even the need for freedom, is an absolute necessity for humankind.

In her book, *No me agarraran viva* (They Won't Take Me Alive), the Salvadoran poet, journalist, and short story writer Claribel Alegría inverts the role of the victim.28 Alegría uses the testimonial voice not in the direct form of a witness to the facts but rather through documents of friends and relatives, by which she recreates the life and death of the Salvadoran guerrilla Eugenia, whose real name was Ana María Castillo Rivas. The book is a fascinating account of the political background of El Salvador's tumultuous history, as well as of the personal history of Eugenia's Christian family, deeply immersed in the pain of their village. The voices of other guerrillas emerge as well, including the voice of Eugenia's husband. The story of the assassination of

Cardinal Romero is also included as part of this story.

Similar to Alegría's completely historical book in that a committed writer lends his or her voice to a cause is a book that mixes history and fiction, *Un día en la vida* (A Day in the Life) by another Salvadoran writer, Manlio Argueta. In this book, Argueta, with a majestic lyricism charged with power, recreates the life of Lupe, a peasant woman from Chalatenango.[29]

Lupe tells about her life, her village, and her shared joys, especially when the men return from hiding. She also gives a first-hand account of the relationship between the peasants and the traditional, conservative church. Her directness is very affecting, as when she confesses that there isn't a God's day she does not get up at five o'clock in the morning and that there isn't a God's day she does not remember the mutilated body of her son, Justino, lying on the highway.

The exploitation of the peasants by the civil guard and internal colonialism are topics that have come to light thanks to the powerful source of testimonial literature. Among the testimonial works of greatest significance in recent years is the text of an indigenous Guatemalan woman from the Province of Quiche, Rigoberta Menchu.[30] Her testimony is without doubt one of the most moving, lyrical, and memorable. Using direct narrative, she tells us:

> My name is Rigoberta Menchu. I am 23 years old. I would like to give you this living testimony that I have not learned in a book and that I have not learned alone, since I have learned all of this with my people, and that is something I want to emphasize.[31]

Again, this testimony is personal and collective. The fact that Menchu had to learn to speak Spanish underlines the double colonization of indigenous people. Menchu's testimony speaks of repression, exploitation by foreign forces, and the abuse of the indigenous population from within the country. For this reason Menchu dedicated herself, at a young age, to becoming a leader of her people and to fighting to eradicate internal colonialism.

This autobiographical book is structured by the voice of Menchu, who learned the language that oppressed her in order to defend herself from it. It is with this same language that we are immersed in a world of magical beliefs. Menchu writes: "I didn't have the opportunity to leave my world, dedicate

myself to myself, so I began to learn to speak Spanish three years ago."[32]
Menchu also discusses the ceremony of birth and the important link between
a person and the earth. This integration with nature is, according to Menchu,
one of the essential components of her world. She also presents a pattern that
has held true since the times of her ancestors: "Many times, the custom in our
culture has made us respect everyone, but they have never respected us."[33]
Menchu's testimonies are full of misery and oppression. These experiences
had a profound effect on her life and shaped her political consciousness.
Throughout the book, she talks to us about the importance of life and about
the culture of life and nature, as opposed to the culture of death:

> The act of killing a person. Death is lived by the rest, be it death by
> accident or in another way. It is something we endure often
> because it is something one feels in one's own flesh. For example,
> the way that my murdered brother died. We don't even like to kill
> an animal. Because we don't like to kill, there isn't violence in the
> indigenous community. For example, the death of a child. If a
> child died from malnutrition, it isn't the parents' fault but because
> of the ladinos conditions. It is a violent act due to the system. Now
> they want us to live in a different way than we want to live. For us,
> killing is something monstrous. From this comes the indignation
> we feel for all the repression, and our devotion to the struggle is
> related to this, to all this suffering we feel.[34]

The nonviolence of the indigenous people stands out in the pages of this
book. It contrasts with the violent oppression of the army that enters the land
of the indigenous inhabitants, takes it from them, burns their houses, rapes
their women, and tortures them. For this reason, the first part of the book is
structured around the ideologies and beliefs of the Guatemalan people, espe-
cially those from the province of Quiche. It is because of certain concrete
experiences like the daily exploitation, and the death of friends and her little
brother, that Menchu joins a guerrila group and becomes an organizer and
defender of her people.

The memoirs of her journeys, the story of a time she was almost captured,
and an account of her stay in a convent of nuns that supported the opposition

forces make Menchu's confessions something that must be read because the reader becomes a participant. This is the true merit in this type of autobiography. The reader cannot remain unperturbed by what is told because, through the text, he or she enters into a world of human brutality and violence.

Through Menchu's testimony, she makes it clear that she is but one of many oppressed people everywhere. Her culture, like others, is besieged by forces that control and violate it. The history of colonialism and repression in the countries of the Third World is underscored not through statistics or the number of dead and missing but through a single voice that, in speaking of others like herself, creates a common history. A beautiful example of the collective work of the people is described in the following scene:

> I had to teach others. For this reason, I went to the most needy community where they were most threatened, where I had friends. We women have a great love for rivers. It is a very beautiful atmosphere when we go down to the river, even if we have to spend the whole day looking for fish among the rocks. But it was a pleasure for me because they were my friends and our friendship was confirmed when we were on the plantations.[35]

The following paragraph defines and explains the feelings of so many captured people:

> The exploitation, the discrimination I have felt in my flesh, the oppression that does not allow us to celebrate our ceremonies and does not respect our way of life. At the same time, they have killed my loved ones, the neighbors I had in my village. I have passed through many places where I have had the opportunity to say something about my village.[36]

In the face of fear and death these testimonies say "no" to silence and to the fate of all the people missing in a subhuman and diabolical world. What would the political history of Argentina have been without the Mothers of the Plaza de Mayo with their white kerchieves embroidered with the initials of their disappeared loved ones? Would the world, so often indifferent and astonished, have learned about the almost 30,000 people who disappeared in Argentina during the "dirty war"? From these spoils, writers, activists, and ordinary citizens constructed a language against authoritarianism, a language that accuses, denounces, and feels; words are the fundamental weapon against indifference, fear, and forgetfulness.

The function of the writer and journalist is to present the truth. Latin America writers have demonstrated that to present the truth is more than an ethical posture for them because they are taking risks that may result in their exile, torture, or death. Many writers have been killed by fascist forces. Others have preferred exile and contribute to the history of their respective countries from the outside. All of them continue to construct new vocabularies that rescue memory and create something beautiful, good, and noble from pain and the most terrible conditions of human existence.

Translated by Janice Molloy

VISION AND TRANSGRESSION:
SOME NOTES ON THE WRITING
OF JULIETA KIRKWOOD

During the decade of the 1970s under Latin American authoritarian govern-
ments, the women of various economic and social strata acquired a very par-
ticular consciousness of their identity as women, citizens and political beings.
Oddly enough, at a time when all official communication channels were
closed, women accustomed to private, invisible tasks found a new way of
"making politics," of bringing their presence to bear in public life—in the
counter-space of the streets and alternative spheres "empowered" by the dicta-
torial regimes.

Julieta Kirkwood, sociologist, political activist and faithful defender of
human rights, began her essay career and became a visible figure during the
military dictatorship in Chile. She was a cultural organizer in women's groups,
fostering unity in the face of a dictatorship that, little by little, immobilized the
role of intellectual women. Her activism centered around a concrete praxis of
the political life on the streets and the popular protests against a culture of
death propagated by the dictatorship. From a direct, testimonial perspective,
Julieta Kirkwood thus began to formulate her theory of the Chilean woman's
way of making politics and history. Over more than a decade of intellectual
engagement, she developed what was to become one of the most important
studies dedicated to women and politics in Chile.

Ser politica en Chile (To be a Political Woman in Chile)[1] constitutes an inter-
esting, alternative text for many reasons. First of all, it differs significantly

from other historical treatises about women and politics in Chile in that Kirkwood gathers a group of writings prepared primarily for FLACSO[2] and written from a radical perspective in which she analyzes the contradictions of women's roles in Chilean political history. She begins with a personal prologue recounting her feminist activism and the vision behind the book:

> We reconstructed the story of what had been invisible and we proposed to break with the private; we were very brave: heretics by dint of shamelessly, openly turning everything around; we discovered, discovered with passion, laughter, tough fights, difficult reflections, we kept going, we opened the Circle [of Women's Studies], the House [of the Woman, called "La Morada," the Dwelling], we opened books, even the Lila Woman's Bookstore; we were crazily daring, I can see it now.

Often writing in an elliptical, lyrical style that captures the transgressive mood of the early 1980s, Kirkwood nonetheless makes it clear what she hopes her writing precipitates:

> With my daring I want to encourage the publication of the hundreds of studies, essays, stories, poems that so many of us women for so long have hidden under our beds or in dark bureaus. We need confrontation and the interplay of ideas wide open to millions of bright thoughts and small ideas.

In the six chapter-essays that follow, Kirkwood offers a feminist perspective of Chilean political history. Not only is her book an informative overview of women's involvement in Chilean politics from the early 1900s to the 1980s, it is a philosophical inquiry on the relationship between political women and authoritarian governments. Kirkwood reconceptualizes the role of the Chilean woman in her battle for suffrage, develops new theories concerning women's participation in institutionalized politics, and examines the relationship between feminist politics and the dictatorship.

Although the fight for women's right to vote began in Chile in the 1920s with success finally achieved in 1949, women remained unable to secure positions in established political parties. Kirkwood describes the heightening consciousness of Chilean women through the years and their more recent efforts to understand their position in a male-dominated society. In particular, she discusses alternative modes for creating, expressing, and considering the history of the Chilean women and their political participation during times of severe political repression when the possibility of political activity was forbidden.

Kirkwood uses a direct and personal language in her book that engages the reader and allows her to experience history first-hand. From the very beginning, Kirkwood establishes a complicity between herself and her reader; history becomes objective and subjective at the same time, allowing for ambiguity in knowledge. In her research on the history of women, Kirkwood reveals that she first investigated official historical records only to discover that the history of Chilean women was far from that expressed by the official story. As she remarks, "As a woman, I'm no stranger to history. I'm not just surfacing now; I've always been there, but in a condition of cold history that appears not to move, not to flow, that has always been necessary and will always be routine to the point that we forget about it until we need it." This quote allows us to understand Kirkwood's unique perspective, which is to write history not simply by annotating the past but by challenging the present as well.

Kirkwood's book clearly reflects her belief that women should convert history into their own story and use it as a tool for political activism. Writing about history, for her, is not a passive task but the creation of another way of being, a new set of rules. In Foucauldian terms, it involves recognizing that every power has a counter-power or, in this case, women's own attempt to achieve their own liberation. To write history is to show their presence, their visibility. And its is also to point out the transformation into subject of a specific social group that has not been completely recognized as such by themselves or by others and up to now has only been a passive receptor of well or poorly formed policies for its attributed human condition.

The fundamental legacy of Kirkwood's historical studies is her belief that an understanding of the past can be transformed into a strong present-day political activism to change the future. For Kirkwood, women's history provides an arena where the personal and the political come together. She expresses how women move in history, how they create it and how they can reconstruct it.

Throughout her book, Kirkwood ponders the relationship of women with their society and its politics. She does not simply write about the established powers, she also creates a dialogue with them. In these conversational, often defiant dialogues, Kirkwood not only discusses history but creates it by her own transgression as one traditionally silenced or marginalized.

For Kirkwood, women's participation or non-participation in the official political parties is a very inaccurate measure of their actual political participation. Consequently she studies women's political activity through the organizations they form independently; for example, the short-lived PFCH (Chilean Feminine Party) which came into being shortly before women's suffrage was achieved and died with a political scandal that would probably have only wounded it had its members had more experience in politics. What is most noteworthy from Kirkwood's viewpoint is the fact that this incident in women's history has been treated as a kind of "family secret," giving the impression that women themselves "tried not only to erase the failure and pain of their defeat,...but also...to deny that it ever occurred." The fact is, women's autonomous political participation as feminists was stifled for decades thereafter for a variety of reasons.

Even the "global liberation" era of the '60s and '70s did not bring about a reassessment of women's role in Chilean political history. Kirkwood advances several hypotheses to explain this, but basically the female question was ignored by Chilean women themselves who, if they were involved in the social liberation movement, did not identify women's liberation as a primordial issue. Their concerns remained subordinated to others because, claims Kirkwood, they lacked the perspective to recognize, analyze, and change their circumstance.

Kirkwood points out that from the very beginning, women's history has been limited to the way men see it. It is time for a new theoretical foundation for Chilean history, she says; it must take into account the "unknown and unrecognized history of women in Chile," not the history of extraordinary women but the record of an ongoing, conscious "feminine demand for the construction of a non-oppressive, non-discriminatory society."

One of the legacies postulated in Kirkwood's philosophy is the importance of everyday life in politics. By everyday life we refer to the incorporation of women's civic participation as an inseparable expression of their identity. This would apply to different classes of women in society who all experience the effects of being marginated from the centers of power. It is Kirkwood's experience as a political activist marching down the streets of Santiago, as well as her link to the rural women's groups, that solidifies her theoretical basis for associating the authoritarianism of the Pinochet government with the recent rise of feminism in Chile and a recognition of the connection between political and domestic authoritarianism. To Kirkwood, the domestic abuse of women is a reflection of the abuses of power being committed under the violent patriarchal seal. Those who would seek to reinstitute democracy without reexamining the whole structure of patriarchal society are separating the public and the private spheres and thereby prolonging the subordination of women. During the military dictatorship, and especially during the 1980s, domestic violence in Chile became rampant, even though this did not appear in official records or newspapers. To Kirkwood, the culture of the dictatorship produced a deep schism and trauma in daily life which magnified the reality of women's lives:

> We women recognize and testify that our daily concrete experience is authoritarianism.Women live—and have always lived—under authoritarianism inside the home, their recognized place of work and experience. What is structured and institutionalized there is precisely the undisputed authority of the father as leader of the family, discrimination and subordination based on gender.

Kirkwood's theories on the relationship between governmental authoritarianism in society at large and patriarchal authoritarianism in the home for women are especially relevant now, as society is going through changes, questioning its values and gaining a new consciousness. For the first time in history, Chilean feminism as a movement has achieved changes for women and a repossession of women's history by women themselves. Kirkwood explains it thus:

> In developing these ideas, we feminists have found that traditional political practice, however women are involved, is segregationist and subordinating in all sociopolitical sectors, whether the women

political actors are shanty-town dwellers, peasants, employees or professionals.

This concept is very important for Julieta Kirkwood because it provides a new explanation for the relationship between women and political parties, demystifying the much-believed theory that defined women according to their social class and concluded that their class alone dictated their political participation. Kirkwood feels that the years of the military dictatorship were a time where Chilean women, seeking justice and peace and a right to political expression, forged for themselves a new identity with a new awareness of their reality both in the political and private spheres.

Before this book was published, the history of women's political participation in Chile was meager and the few treatises, like Felicitas Klimpel's text, focused on the traditional reading of history from and about the patriarchal model. By 1992, Kirkwood's book had gone into its third edition and has become an indispensable literary work for all feminist discussions in Chile and other parts of Latin America. There are not many reviews of this book; the recognition it has achieved has been mainly by word-of-mouth, through encounters between women who recommended its reading. The text is brief and does not present the history of women's participation in Chilean politics in a traditional linear fashion, nor does it exhaust the topic since many aspects of women's history are not covered. We would define this essay with Kirkwood's words from the book's cover, as "a feminist reading of our history. It is a history to be discussed, to be doubted, to be reflected upon, to give us back our lives."

We could establish an interesting parallel with what Kirkwood says about the image of "life being cut." The military dictatorship annihilated the socialization and the identity of women that had begun with the socialist reforms of Salvador Allende. It is during times of crisis and deep dilemmas that visionary leaders among women take the stage. Among them can be counted Julieta Kirkwood, who understood the possibility of women's existence through alternate means, through informal gatherings around potluck dinners and other seemingly non-subversive events, where the common bonds shared under the oppressive dictatorship were born and where Kirkwood began to reflect about women's political role in Chile.

One document she consulted on women's suffrage was the 1952 text by Elena Caffarena entitled *Un capitulo en la historia del feminismo* (A Chapter in the History of Feminism). Kirkwood repossessed the voice of women like Elena Caffarena and then investigated magazines of the period in order to sketch the invisible and alternate history of Chilean women. It is interesting to note that most footnotes and quotes in Kirkwood's book originate in unpublished documents, fliers, speeches found in libraries. This technique makes her work a research that rescues but also that values thoughts that had not been valued or not fully formed. This is why Kirkwood's thoughts occasionally seem fragmented .

Julieta Kirkwood's book reached the public at that crucial time in Chile's history when Chilean women began to question the relationship between their identity and their gender. *Ser política en Chile* was published posthumously and Kirkwood never knew the wide resonance it would have. Her presence and vitality deeply touched those who knew her in her lifetime, and this was without any doubt her most enduring contribution.

Translated by Monica Bruno

Inhabitants
of Decayed Palaces:
The Dictator in the Latin American Novel

When the Sandinista troops entered the palace of Anastacio Somoza, the press noted that an empty uniform remained flung across the elegant sofa of the opulent home of the dictator. The image of that empty uniform, nearly devoid of history but more so, of human life, appears to be a recurring metaphor in a number of texts. The dictator, either imagined or real, is a central theme in contemporary Latin American literature and forms part of an established canon.[1]

Certain recurring images, as well as techniques of language and narration, are utilized to show, historically or mythically, the almost hyperbolic figure of the dictator that forms an integral part of the Latin American cultural ideology. The concept of gender and authority have an important role in how the dictator is presented.

The 1970s was a crucial decade when authoritarian governments in Latin America erupted with overwhelming force. At the same time, the "boom" of Latin American literature took place in many parts of the Western world. Clearly, these novels may have emerged for all the same historical and social reasons that make the resurgence of a dictator possible. Nevertheless, a more complex reason than the historical causes exists; reasons linked to experimentation with a new language and writing style.[2]

Alejo Carpentier's *Reasons of State*, Roa Bastos' *I, the Supreme* and Garcia Marquez' *Autumn of the Patriarch,* all published in the '70s, are three novels in which the myth of authority, almost simultaneously, appears as a theme. In *I, the Supreme* this myth acts as a destructive entity through language whose spacial images allude to this idea of destruction in fiction.

The antecedents to those novels discuss the dictator as if he were still the supreme patriarch, as in Miguel Angel Astruias' novel, *El Senor Presidente,* and *Amalia* by Jose Marmol. These two novels support the traditional concept of the dictator as the supreme, omnipotent figure of authority who controls everything through the use of words and who appears everywhere in overt and covert ways. Curiously, in *El Senor Presidente* the face of the supreme patriarch remains invisible; he is the hidden figure that is able to appear anywhere, causing terror in everyone.

Autumn of the Patriarch was, in the opinion of many critics, one of Garcia Marquez's most successful novels. In an unrestrained manner of writing, the novel addresses the theme of power and hyperbolic writing. The demythification of the dictator begins with the discovery of a body at the entrance to the palace, where the amorphous corpse had lived. The image of the discarded uniform here resonates with true history:

> Over the weekend the vultures got into the presidential palace by pecking through the screens on the balcony windows and the flapping to their wings stirred up the stagnant time inside and at dawn on Monday the city awoke out of its lethargy of centuries with the warm, soft breeze of a great man dead and rotting in grandeur. Only then did we dare go in without attacking the crumbling walls of reinforced stone, as the more resolute had wished, and without using oxbows to knock the main door off its hinges, as others had proposed, because all that was needed was for someone to give a push and the great armored doors that had resisted the lombards of William Dampier during the building's heroic days gave way.[3]

The entire novel, written in an uninterrupted monotone as if propelled by a deep breath, carries the reader toward the discovery of the body of the dictator, a body that will be almost impossible to identify since the patriarch has a double. In addition, when the body is found it is decomposed, making identification impossible and adding to the continuous confusion.

A game of mirrors permeates the writing of the text. On one hand, the dictator is invisible and the habit of seeing him has been lost. On the other hand, if he is seen, it is not him that we are seeing. It is as if the story of the *Autumn of the Patriarch* is based on the search for a lost body. This is also an interesting parallel that recalls certain similarities with the current political history of Latin America where the families of the "disappeared" search desperately for the body of a lost person.

Narration without any type of pause allows the reader to become totally absorbed within the waves of sounds. We, the readers, are part of this search, as well as judges who observe scenes, especially when we enter the palace and find a decomposing body. With the clarity of a videocamera, we view the scene, along with the author of the text, who also takes part in the desperate search of the palace. At the time of the encounter, the dictator is already defeated and the reader enters the palace in the same way that the Sandinista forces entered in search of Somoza.

I, the Supreme by Augusto Roa Bastos brings the degree of demythification in writing to a still higher level than that of Garcia Marquez. Roa Bastos continuously plays with the ambiguity of writing as well as with his power to recreate it. Roa Bastos does not choose a setting of mythic dictators in remote Caribbean countries as does Garcia Marquez. His text is situated in a very precise location, Paraguay, with a historical figure, Dr. Francia. Nevertheless, in spite of creating a text closely based on historical documents, the Paraguayan author builds a brilliant and speculative theory around the character in question.

The presentation of concrete facts, such as the writings of Dr. Francia himself, makes this novel distinct from the concept of fiction. Here, Roa Bastos assumes that history, as recreated through his writing, does not belong to him as author, but to the actual, official chronological history of Paraguay. In great part, the book is formed by the personal memoirs of Dr. Francia and includes memoirs of those opposed to him as well as the translations of such eccentric characters as two British merchants.

The most interesting part of the text is the inclusion of footnotes. The voice of the writer describing the formation of the book appears in the footnotes. The elaboration of the notes and the composition of the collage converts Roa Bastos into a type of a judge who verifies what has happened by means of the ordering of his writing. He also invites us to think about the numerous versions and revisions of the correct, official history as being like that of the text.

The use of a scribe who arranges the memoirs is the essential factor in the game between the author, his own writing, and the veracity of the historical figure of the patriarch. Every act of ordering and cataloging already implies a certain degree of judgment and revision. In this way, the text of I, the Supreme participates in demythification to a much greater degree still than the work of Garcia Marquez because the writing itself is demystified. Speculations about the language and the importance of speech are the central characteristics of El Supremo. It is one book in which the importance of written language is highlighted with absolute clarity. This emphasis is used to arrange the texts in opposition to the fascination of the dictator with the spoken quality of language which makes him capable of participating in the transformation of history.

At the end of El Supremo's life, in one of his rare moments of weakness, he confesses to his dog, Sultan, that he fears losing the power to be able to speak, thus losing all possibility of controlling communication. Initially, the scribe Patino is the only one capable of copying down the memoirs of Dr. Francia, and the writer becomes the real judge of the monstrosities of the dictator.

In 1983, the journalist Tomas Eloy Martinez used the same method as Roa Bastos, remaking history and creating a novel by using newspaper clippings, interviews, and the memoirs of Don Juan Domingo Peron. In an interview with Eloy Martinez, he confessed that if he were truly devoted to writing a work about Peron and what really occurred during his years in government, he would not be able to because the audience would believe that it was all a lie. Therefore, he decided to write fiction by means of history, utilizing, as Roa Bastos did, a scribe, this time not fictionalized like Patino, but the true-to-life figure of the terrible Lopez Rega, follower of astrology and the occult and guilty of many acts of perversity.[4]

The Peron Novel, in its reading and its metaphoric meanings, is still more complex than I, the Supreme owing to constant changes of space and unities of time. The book takes place during Peron's trip in 1973 from Madrid to Buenos Aires, a trip that lasts exactly eighteen hours. The number of hours is the precise equivalent of the years of dictatorship and of Peron's exile.

The demythification of this complex dictator who was so loved by the factions of the extreme right as well as of the left occurs the moment that he boards the plane, worn out, weakened, without even knowing the true reasons for his return. Throughout the book, as Juan Peron reconstructs his life, we observe not only constant allusions to the life of the dictator but also to the way in which this same life begins to grow feeble, to fade because the dictator begins to doubt his history as well as his power. Upon his return to Buenos Aires, the crowd waits for Peron with enthusiasm while the elderly dictator, sickly and debilitated, is hardly able to descend from the airplane. The book ends with the following sentence: "Resurrect Big Man! What is to stop you?"[5]

All these texts, from the work of Gabriel Garcia Marquez to the most recent of Tomas Eloy Martinez, point toward a very basic structure and elaboration of the language, as well as to the decentralization of power by means of language.

Garcia Marquez describes in *The Autumn of the Patriarch*'s continuous search for the dictator's body the invisibility of power, and therefore, its precariousness. The whole book is composed as if it were an immense text, empty and doleful, as if in the writing the breath was lost. By not using any type of punctuation, this incessant, perpetual search for power is made even more overwhelming. The preoccupation with language is associated with the vigilant preoccupation with the truth that is constantly beaten down under dictatorial regimes.

Beyond language, the texts in which the figure of a dictator is the focal point highlight another theme linked with power: memory. *From Autumn of the Patriarch* to *The Peron Novel,* the protagonists constantly suffer from spacial lapses and digressions of the memory. Many of them make use of a secretary that acts as a judge and orders the pronouncements of power. In the act of creating a new order, the autonomous memory of the dictators, protagonists, and readers is also altered.

These texts involves motifs of recovery as well as of loss. Recovery born in the search for lost bodies is a metaphor regarding bodies devoid of power and implies, as well, a new form of reading. Therefore, one is not able to read these books in a linear, orderly fashion, and the reader must invent and reconstruct in imagination these demented and marvelous figures. To read these texts is to participate in a game that attempts to unmask and expose power and to recover it through a process that the reader begins to make his own.

In two short stories by Garcia Marquez, "Big Mama's Funeral" and "The Incredible and Sad Tale of Innocent Erendira," the figure of the female dictator appears. The theme of feminine power is an interesting one due to the opposing forces in Latin America between women and political and sexual power, but Garcia Marquez is one of the few authors who devote time to the study of this theme. He also uses language in a very interesting way when portraying the female dictator, a language that moves away from conventional rhetoric and portrays the female dictator in a highly lyrical style.

In contrast to *The Autumn of the Patriarch,* the female dictator in "Big Mama's Funeral" is depicted in a concrete manner. She is rubicund, of flesh and blood; she is real. We are not forced to search for her body. The language in the story ranges from festive to lyrical and the reader many times feels that Big Mama is a generous and kind figure. Her possessions are described with humor and her actions appear almost beneficent, something that never happens with the figures of the other dictators. The concept of power is totally opposite to that of the deteriorating dictator. Her subjects love her and cry for her after her death, or at least pretend to. Her corpulent figure is not terrifying. Above all, an exquisite sense of humor permeates the text and the subtext.

The feminization of power is described in a humorous way, and the political aspect is connected to the everyday because death does not come by torture but through taxes. Cheating and bribery are everyday facts. In the story of Erendira, the authoritarian figure is embodied by the mother/grandmother who exploits her own granddaughter and prostitutes her to obtain her own pleasure.

These portraits of female autonomy and domination are very different from authoritarian, masculine power. Such characters occur in the bonds of the family in small villages that distance the inhabitants from the big cities. For example, Erendira's story takes place in the desert. What is Garcia Marquez suggesting through these stories? That women exercise anomalous power differently than men? That authoritarianism varies and each time becomes something different? When power is exercised by women, why is the tone colloquial and comical? Perhaps it is an attempt to demythify authoritarian power by expressing it with great humor. These questions do not have definitive answers, only the reader's reactions to this new vision of the female.

What happens with the feminine author who elects to raise questions concerning themes of authority and control? Up until now there have appeared two important texts in which the horrors of dictatorship are discussed. They are not centered around one figure in particular but instead focus on the sensations and experiences of a nation plunged into a fascist state.

Marta Traba in *Mothers and Shadows* chooses the interior monologue in the secrecy of an apartment in the center of Buenos Aires. The space is clandestine, censorious, and silent. It is a place where voices of horror are heard, where bodies of the tortured are visualized in the regions of the Southern Cone: Argentina, Chile, and Uruguay. The narration is by two women from different generations reunited by one of the causalities of a common destiny. Irene, once a prestigious actress, lost her daughter in a concentration camp. She reunites with Dolores, the youngest victim of the repression and the symbol of torture and the loss of innocence, as well as the loss of an entire generation. The power in *Mothers and Shadows* resides in the horrors of seeing everyday life tinted with political violence and despair.

Scenes of the Mothers of the Plaza de Mayo circling the pyramid in the plaza, frantically searching for the victims of the repression, are images that readers appropriate and make their own. Again, the power is not represented under the common denominator of a malevolent, destructive figure in absolute control of everything; the repression goes beyond the simple construction of a mythic figure. The repression, the fear, the pain, the immense sadness, the violence surface in daily life and, above all, in the specters of those that remain, of those that survive. Irene states:

And what a hell, Dolores! A new man-made version, such as no one ever imagined. Without a word or command being uttered, the women raised the photographs above their heads. Why, when there was no one there to see them? I expected that with so much handling and fondling those childlike faces would soon be disfigured past the point of recognition. Near me, an old woman was holding up a cheap, studio portrait with both hands. The girl was smiling stiffly, her head tilted to one side, no doubt obeying the photographer's instructions. She was sitting with her legs crossed, an organdy dress covering her knees. Another woman was holding

a passport photograph in the palm of her hand, shielding it as if it
were an egg she'd just that minute hatched; she raised it gingerly
and started to wave it from side to side; she couldn't stop shaking
and the tears were streaming down her face, but she kept her lips
tightly pressed together.[6]

In *For the Fatherland*[7] the young writer Diamela Eltit employs the fear, the
terror, as well as the torture and the love of the tortured ones, in order to
describe what happens to the inhabitants of a city submerged under a neofas-
cist dictatorship. *For the Fatherland* is the story of sieges and deaths, narrated
by a series of voices, especially that of Coya, the central protagonist of the
Santiago neighborhood. The terror and the fear is perceived in the signs of
hunger in the bodies of those who prostitute themselves for a bit of bread, as
well as in the language that Eltit utilizes to exemplify the indifference of these
characters. Eltit includes a collection of clearly real testimonies in which tor-
ture and the repression of the lower spheres of society, engulfed in the
absence of relationships and also submerged in a profound hopelessness and
sense of uprootedness, is clearly depicted.

Mothers and Shadows and *For the Fatherland* are stories of women under dic-
tatorships, women from different classes and experiences. The phenomenon
of power is perceived and sensed in the everyday experiences, in the com-
plaints, in the dread that occurs with the arrival of the nighttime and that
destroys everyone and everything.

The woman writer has focused her denunciation not on the mythic figure
of the dictator, but on the terror of each day—terror that levels and destroys
households, neighborhoods, and above all, the very core of being of each per-
son. If the metaphor of the discovery of a tortured body as a symbol of the
immensity of imposed power occurs frequently in these novels, the woman
writes of the power and its consequences to the families of the disappeared.
The insistence on finding the body of the destroyer is translated into an insis-
tence on rescuing the body that cries out from hunger or from torture. The
language used fluctuates between the lyrical and the stark visions of women
still searching for bread or for refuge from those who persecute them. Diamela
Eltit, like Marta Traba, employs the lyrical, experimenting with sounds to
express pain as well as to create images of love: a hand that clutches and

searches. These women challenge power through the voices of those who remain to denounce and to judge.

Translated by Barbara E. Pierce

PASSION AND MEMORY
WOMEN WRITERS IN LATIN AMERICA

It is possible through the written word to draw close to memory. In moments of luminosity, the intensity of a poem, the polyphony of its sounds, or the unforgettable protagonist meandering over the pages of a novel, may be transformed into a voice which articulates memory. Chris Wallace Crabb, an Australian poet, states in *Falling into Language* (Oxford Unversity Press), "All works of literature are to an extent acts of retrieval. Life escapes, it is lost and the writer erects, creates a verbal substitute on paper, a complexity of gestures adding up to a larger, former gesture which is time regained. Not for nothing do writers keep journals and notebooks. These are the halfway houses between life and letters."

Farther back in time than Homer's *Odyssey*, and throughout literature and history, the process of spilling out the coffers of memory as written words has been far and away a masculine one. Women have been missing persons on this pilgrimage. They have been the keepers of secret recollections, authors of epistles that were censored or had to be kept hidden away. Out of necessity, they forged a new way of remembering and of recreating memory.

In the process of thinking about the journey of memory, we must pause and reflect upon forgetting because forgetting eradicates memory. To speak of forgetting, we must also speak of denial, and denial is one of the most common practices evidenced in Latin American culture in the past twenty years. Those of my generation have become the custodians of memory. We are the ones who converse with the ghosts of the disappeared.

As women we both are and are not the voices of those who shouted the names of detained individuals or kept those names a secret.. We were the ones who vacillated between telling and not telling, between silence and a scream. Over the past twenty years, Latin American ideological discourse has centered around remembering and forgetting, between the symbolism of the body as firsthand witness and the body of the disappeared, which proves absence and loss.

To speak of memory is to speak of the history it articulates. Journals and orally-transmitted messages have formed part of those preeminent texts which have transmitted te history of Latin America, as well as the corpus of Latin American imagination. These texts, according to José Narváez Pehuén in *La Invención de la Memoria*, "are able to experience a legality of spirit situated along the margins." In other words, they give validity to the experiences of those whose circumstance has made them illegitimate, eccentric, undervalued, classified without identity in libraries, and placed in an ambiguous and miscellaneous category within literary histories. These reflections by Narárez lead to the subject of women writers, who have existed within marginality and outside the perimeters of established canon space, and whose work is the sum and sustance of discourse and discord. Narváez enlarges upon the theoretical point of view of documentary discourse, whose purpose must be to inform, to tell, and also to recognize the presence of "the other." Any preface to Latin American discourse that endeavors to name, thus creating the imaginary and the fantastic, also has to do with the process of bearing witness, of telling, of saying, and not contradicting. The necessity of writing an epistle or generating from it the chronicles of history are part of the Latin American cultural legacy.

Such a discourse must include chronicles, memoirs, travel and childhood diaries, logbooks and news articles, all of which form part of the social knowledge and totality of Latin American experience. These are the subtexts of history and the confabulation of fiction writing. However, they are also diversified works which dialogue with a state of absence. Narváez's meditations force us to think about women's texts, letters, missives, and travel diaries, such as the first Chilean text written by a woman: María Graham, the wife of a British captain who arrived on the coast of Valparaíso. Her *Diario de una residencia en Chile* (1820) expresses a woman's experience. Why does she write? How will women's writing be recognized within that duplicitous anomaly of being a woman and a foreigner?

Since the Latin American collective imagination celebrates orality and the articulation of literature as witness, elements of that primary literary substructure continue to be shaped by the invention of what Hispanic America is, and, thus, must include women, whose voices, though in the mists, are unequivocal. The parlance of women writers is often tied to the testimonial discourse and autobiography found within the texts of apologie from the seventeenth century, such as the concise and powerful autobiography of Sor Juana Inés de la Cruz. The autobiography of the prioress centers upon access to knowledge and wisdom. Other autobiographical writings are centered around the voice of a confessor, a voice which represents authority and obliges women to write and confess. With the exception of convent discourse, women did not actually write autobiography; their lives and identities were part of the cultural scenario. Women wrote letters and travel diaries, but these were the exceptions; apart from the writings of María Graham and Flora Tristan, there were no women's texts which recorded their lives and deeds.

Latin American women's autobiographical writing has been silenced. At times, figures such as Venezuelan Teresa de la Parra, the Countess of Merlín in Cuba, and Emilia Pardo Bazán in Spain, emerged as writers of autobiography, but these epistolary texts were linked with scandal and did not appear until the nineteen seventies. In *Memory of Mamá Blanca,* de la Parra elaborates upon the bourgeois childhood of a wealthy Latin American girl. The countess of Merlín touches upon a story of exile and a baroque Cuban paradise. Both of these women's autobiographical journeys are essentially masculine: they wrote in compliance with what was expected of women. De la Parra tells a story of lovelessness, idleness and boredom; the countess speaks of an exotic and well-to-do world, both in and out of Cuba.

Let us reflect upon the phenomenon of women's literary production during the decade of the seventies and its connection to the autobiographical text. The era of political violence and military dictatorship in the Southern Cone countries established a new style of writing with an alternative vision underscoring the image of women and their writing. If during colonial times authority is represented in the figure of the confessor, in the twentieth century the confessor is censor whose power is weakened by women who imagine his way of speaking.

Who writes about women? How does one write about women? How do we collect the places of memory which constitute one of the most essential confines of current feminine personal discourse? The sixties decade denoted a return to orality, to the appreciation of that which is uncultured and the documentation of everyday life. Studies on domesticity and compendiums about the lives of women servants and farm laborers also began to appear. During the seventies, women chose marginalization and the voice of the dispossessed as autobiographical text, often searching for the hidden and anonymous voice of unspoken poverty to draw closer to the voice of the reader. They sought the voice of the silenced, the sequestered, and of what was irredeemably lost. Elena Poniatowska in her book *"Hasta no verte Jesús mío"* (Until I see you my Jesus) not only set down a way of creating and documenting the testimony of a marginalized woman but legitimized the disenchanted voices of all women who live in poverty. Aren't the writings of Victoria Ocampo, in which she is the autobiographical object and speaks of her condition as a wealthy woman in search of a renowned voice also the ever-privileged voice of disobedience and rebellion? The phenomenon of "underprivileged testimony" experienced a great upturn beginning in the seventies when women writers undertook the huge task of gathering oral texts which were not necessarily lost, as was the case in the sixties with attempts to recover the writings of María Luisa Bombal, Silvina and Victoria Ocampo, and Teresa de la Parra.

The speech of intimate and popular discourse is born out of the decentralized marginality of she who writes. The entire era of silence and repression of voice is what determines the onset of limited speech. The articulation that began with those same testimonial voices which had sprung up in the seventies and continued into the last part of the eighties decade is one which is homemade. This is true not only of written discourse but also of the creation of the object that is generated and in the materials used, such as leftover or discarded items. An alliance comes into being which brings forth the living history of poverty from the paraphernalia of poverty. History is rooted in the voice which defies and disarticulates voice itself, experience, and the hearing of that suppressed voice, unyielding and secret.

During the military dictatorship in Chile, journals of women's writing were begun. *Lavando La Esperanza* (Washing Hope) was started by a group of laundresses from Santiago. In Bolivia, a collection of writings by female domestic workers made its appearance. In many regions, life stories were constructed within a society that silenced these women by reason of class, gender, or ideology. These women created themselves in their own authentic or "home-made" language.

Since the 1920s, women's autobiography has been the patrimony of economically privileged women, and their stance as crazy, deluded, and exceptional lead them to penetrate the zones of unofficial discourse. Paradoxically, the autobiographical writing which carries weight is that of women slum-dwellers. These women, in the face of authority and out of their own experiences of austerity and disarticulation of language, created their own story in order to survive. Slum-dwelling women express their condition out of a desire to give testimony. In their spontaneity, these women theorize about the meaning of discussing their own actions from a practical vantage point.

Alongside autobiographical writing in grassroots communities, in laundries, and in poor sectors, voices of women rise forth. Literature ceases to be the story of the masculine, heroic experience, of nobility or power. Women now place themselves within the regions of orality, and this orality transforms itself into the vocation and task of women writers.

Through which seam, through which thimble does the memory of women pass? In "Women and Testimony: Some Critical Reflections" (*The Invention of Memory*), Sonia Montecinos states, "Out of the seduction of her open lips, women will recreate a memory which will pour everlastingly upon her loved ones, upon the 'others,' and upon the world."

Latin American women's testimonial writing shares the circumstance of of a nebulous existence, of never having been part of the scenario, or part of official cultural discourse. Women begin to express an atavistic sense of memory from that same fundamental experience of narrating. How, then, to go about remembering? The answer lies in written recollection in combination with the necessity of documenting rituals and sacred events. Indigenous women narrate from the vantage point of harvests, of mythical communion with the earth up to the time of pain, of breaking away, and of exile from agrarian living to urban life.

All autobiographies of indigenous women, the one by Rigoberta Menchú being the most well known, propose a world vision based on prayer, ceremony, and the sacred word, which is as much her own history as it is that of the community. The point of departure of all that "being" and "inhabiting" the world comes from the sacred and almost secret origin of their status as members of an ethnic group where personal history is rooted in the history of the collective. This writing generates a cultural identity which is both communal and individual and differs from other autobiographical voices, such as those of de la Parra and Ocampo. However, this discourse also generates a new way of communicating and a new cultural model.

The oral discourse of these indigenous women proceeds from an intimate region that approaches memory. Woman's experience is intrinsically linked to fragmented discourse and molded into collages with lapses where the reader needs to pay close attention to understand that which is not remembered, cannot be told, or has not been told.

Women's texts are created from intimate family involvement, maternity, and memory, yet neither is more important than the other. Their truths, like their stolen identities, are built of those fragments which recover the authenticity of a devaluated and violated sense of self.

The proliferation of these texts and the testimonies of women farm laborers, housewives and domestic workers underscore the concept of recovery, forgetting, silence, and the devaluation of those tasks which are relevant to femininity. It is necessary to rethink what the concept of silence means. The silence of these women does not have its origins in any sort of shyness, unless someone takes this written word and makes it an object for marketingand mass consumption. Many intermediary voices have attempted to recover literary works from what was not said and from silence. These voices struggle because of the presence of a hierarchy and a literary officialdom that includes the reader.

More than embracing the awareness of women who write, life stories are a ritual act where the presence of otherness is recognized. It is also a place where the person who reads that "other voice" feels different and estranged from the boundaries of power. And it is by virtue of this sense of foreignness and out of experience, that the reader creates and looks at his or herself. Even if the individual does not recognize his or herself, something is learned about the diversity of that other voice. This is one of the reasons why Rigoberta Menchú is an authentic figure par excellence in the multicultural arena. Over and above Menchu's "raised consciousness," her text takes in the zones of ritual and word, the holocaust, indigenous people of five hundred years ago, and dictatorship. Her words bring us closer to that primordial and silenced life. It is fascinating to observe the engendering of autobiographical narratives and stories which appeared years after the production of testimonial texts in Latin America. Rigoberta Menchú's testimony represents a complex ambiguity that lies between textual pronouncement as recovery and forced silence. In the United States, Rigoberta Menchú has been criticized as the standard bearer of multicultural liberalism. She has been accused of wearing her indigenous garb only when she speaks in public. In the reduced literary circles of North American society, her book reinvents the mute dialogue between liberals and fundamentalists. The attention given Menchú's book has intensified its vast circulation and has made the silence of other testimonies become more eloquent. The fact that Rigoberta Menchú's book is read by a small group of people in North American universities makes accusations that Menchú is sensationalistic absurd. Here it is fitting to remember that within the massive reappropriation of women's voices of that time, Menchú's voice is one of many.

In several fields of study there exists a near obsessive desire to learn about Jewish immigration to Latin America. Recently, historians have written books about the Jews in Argentina and Cuba. Note for example, the books *Argentina and the Jews* (Haim Avay, University of Alabama Press) and *Tropical Diaspora* (J. Lesser, University of Florida Press). This phenomena fills the silent void of the history of Jews in Latin America. In that same manner, women reclaim the testimony of their ancestors and the life blood of their lineage. Here, no intermediaries or compilers exist. The author herself speaks, and she gathers the voices of her ancestors.

Amidst this proliferation of texts, which are essentially autobiographies, memoirs, episodes from the past, and tales of love and happiness by and about Jewish women, México has occupied the seat of honor. Curiously, the components of alienism and anti-semitism do not appear as basic elements. What is recreated in these writings are issues of immigration, desires that touch upon the complicity of being while at the same time not being part of a country or its history. With her book, *Genealogies,* (Joaquín Mortiz, 1983), Margo Glantz began a literature which places within it the history of Judaism in Latin America.

Judaism is part of the theme of *mestizaje,* and the confluence of multiple languages and geographies into a single territory. This is the new *mestizaje* of the nineties. Reflecting upon Jewish women writers' relationship to testimonial texts and orality reveals that the recently vindicated right of speech and history came out of the Diaspora in much the same way that women domestic workers come to the city and write about their lives after twenty years of adaptation.

The history of women who write is precarious in the sense that their access to a universal or collective speech has been devaluated and considered to be subversive. Jewish women's writing fills an enormous historical void as far as otherness is concerned. Quite often, Latin American Jewish identity has been usurped, lessened, and absent, as evidenced in the texts of Jewish women writers. These texts and life histories propose ways in which different ethnic communities, such as those of Jewish, Arab, or Yugoslav origin, attempt to incorporate themselves into otherness. At the same time, they try to define identity and its circumstance. More significantly, they reveal how they imagine themselves and how, through writing, they have found themselves. Latin American Jewish writers who have assumed their identity as Jewish writers are scarce. Curiously, women have been the ones to completely assume such an identity.

What were Jewish women writers in Latin America doing? How were they writing as they crossed several oceans and wrote travel diaries about their stays in the places to which they immigrated? Despite the fact that the Jewish community has been aware of how to approach orality by reason of the Diasporas, very little is known about the Jewish experience in Latin America. Jewish women have known how to preserve custom. Rituals, recipes, and prayers have been passed down from mother to daughter, but stories of migrations have barely been recorded. They are stories of silence, distant brush strokes of a history yet to be told.

During the 1980s and early 1990s, something unprecedented appeared in Latin American literature: the Jewish voice. This term acquired a multidimensional perspective during a time when literary works were produced and woven together by voices of Jewish women who wrote about their community. They retold history from distinct vantage points whether through fable, autobiography, or certain pivotal themes, which include migrations in the midst of perpetual wars and Diasporas.

The paradigm of Jewish women writers has always been fascinating and unique. Stories evolve which are oral and almost ritual in nature. The sacred takes on a magical sense, as if the scenes of pre- and post-Holocaust Europe could be transported to the bright landscapes of the tropics of South America. For the most part, the writings of Jewish women are the work of those who belong to privileged class. Middle-class women retrieved and made known the voices of their ancestors, women who came to America in second-class compartments aboard ships. They tell and strengthen ties with other women who tell. And they also reclaim the ancestral loom of the lost voices of those travelers.

Mexico and Argentina have the largest Jewish communities in Latin America. In *Genealogies*, Mexican writer Margo Glantz assumes the identity of a daughter who tells the imaginary and symbolic story of her father. As she narrates, she also speaks about the history of Mexico, living, inventing, and making it her own. Trotsky and Frida Kahlo appear in the book, as do Margo Glantz and her father, she as a writer, he as a poet., both of them Jewish Mexicans, Mexican Jews.

After the publication of Glantz's text, other women reaffirmed their ethnic groups and histories. For example, Elena Poniatowska wrote her autobiography, *La For de Lis,* from the standpoint of her mother's experiences, journeys, and crossings from France to Mexico. Later, Barbara Jacobs wrote *Las Hojas Muertas* (The Dead Leaves), where she retold the story of her Lebanese-Mexican father. These women assumed their identity from a perspective of ethnicity and remote ancestral space. The mothers and fathers, and the life stories themselves, acquired a testimonial voice.

Curiously, in *Genealogies* an exclusive kind of literature is produced which in and of itself narrates the ways in which, vis a vis her father, Margo Glantz commences to participate in the Mexican dialogue and its historical recollections. The book does not center around exclusivity; rather, it articulates ways in which Jews become integrated into the essence of Mexico and the New World. Images of the Holocaust, the Diaspora, and loss are not framed with the same sense of profoundness and anguish as in the texts of Angelina Muniz Huberman, an exceptional Mexican women writer who does not use autobiography as her vehicle of expression. Huberman speaks about her Judaism with a subtle obsession. However, she also manages to include the medieval era, that time of alchemy when the secrets of the universe did not reside in perfection and harmony but in the notion of a mixture of changing elements and the joining together of fate and faith.

Of all the texts on the issue of Jewish identity in Mexico—*Genealogies* by Margo Glantz; *La Bobe,* an autobiographical text by Sabina Berman about the relationship between a granddaughter and her grandmother; and *No Que Te Vea,* (I can't really see you), a book about Rosa Nizzan's childhood; Huberman's text, *Reflexiones Sobre el Antisemitismo* (Reflections on Antisemitism) is perhaps the one which more deeply defines what Jean Paul Sartre called, "the Jewish condition." The book illustrates how a Jewish woman writer situates herself in the world. It points out her relationship with Latin America, her approach to the Diaspora, and the way in which she converses with the past and with the dead. In the field of Hispanic American letters, Huberman possesses incomparable originality.

Huberman's *El Huerto Cerrado* (The Closed Orchard) is one of the most canonical, decisive, and beautiful texts on the Jewish question. All events transpire from the point of view of a closed garden or orchard, where a sense of being converges with identity through literature. The orchard is quiet and enclosed. It is a place where medieval literature joins together with the secrets of the cabala and of alchemy and it moves beyond literary and historical experience. This is an orchard of mysticism. Therefore, it is secret and ambiguous, rooted in all the vocations of mystery. Huberman calls these texts transmutations. And like a good alchemist, she travels and makes a "pilgrimage" in order to get closer to the memory of others. This crucial text creates the story of others journeying through realms both imagined and real, through that great book of life where memory resides.

Huberman's stories, such as "Christian Gentleman" or "The Portuguese Synagogue," are impressive because for her, the Jewish question is one of otherness, of exile and *mesitzaje,* of what comes from the outside, the cornerstone of existence. Through the kaleidoscope of her own questions on racism, she explores the meaning of the Jewish question. In "Brief World" Huberman speaks about the Holocaust and concentration camps, those cities where "they say that not even butterflies flew and flowers did not grow. And in that place there were no trees or birds that could find a place to nest, as if they might have suspended their flight in the face of the unknown, as if water and air kept silent. As if life ended and a cosmic paralysis wandered around as a threat." When Huberman, a forsaken Jew, speaks about her stories, she invokes clairvoyants, magicians, and children condemned to history and a time of hell. "This is the uniform of the children who populate the gray houses of the camp surrounded in barbed wire, guarded by soldiers in high black boots from gray towers".

Alicia Steimberg and Ana Maria Shua of Argentina wrote about their identity as writers before their Mexican counterparts. They wrote from the vantage point of immigration, exile, and ocean crossings.

Without a doubt Ana Maria Shua is one of the most outstanding Argentine Jewish writers. In 1994 she published *El Libro de los Recuerdos* (The Book of Memories).in which she revealed what it was like to be an immigrant family in Argentina. She talked about her immigrant grandparents, who somehow erred, coming to a mistaken America, to South America, not to that desired and powerful one in the north.

Shua speaks about harmony and lovelessness; life's scandals, both large and small; colorful men and passionate women. What is interesting and moving about this book is the fact that it poses the unwavering question of how, when, and why memories are created. Shua is able to do this with the voice of the narrator and an obsessive preoccupation with remembrance. The book repeatedly affirms the way in which history is articulated, how it is written, and what will or will not be included in the text. The *Book of Memories* tells the life stories of other women. These are women from rural areas who tell their story, women who compile stories and select certain codes and messages in order to remember. Both groups, illiterate women and affluent women writers who write about themselves, know that the only trustworthy boundary is the one which belongs to literature and the everyday spoken word. Shua reminds us: "The Book of Memories is the only source which is absolutely reliable. It is easy to get mad at it because it tells the truth, but it never says everything, and it never even says enough."

This brief observation by Shua advances themes central to these reflections and powerfully articulates the idiom of the sacred and mythic which are the rituals of all remembrance. The testimonial literature dealt with in these writings offers up the dialectic in question as game, myth, metaphor and the transfiguration of patterns. Here, memory, recollection, desire and forgetting are voiced along with the historic periods to which they belong.

The end of the book, where Shua remembers a time of fear and terror, might be compared to certain short stories by Angelina Huberman where she speaks about the horror camps where nothing blooms, where everything is gray and sinister and falls into ruin. Literature is the other face of shadow. It is through words that we bloom.

All Jewish migration to Latin America was marked by fear and access to little known and unexpected spheres, and Shua underscores this fear with even greater intensity at the time of the dictatorship. That same fear shares explicit resonance with the terror produced by the holocaust: "What was worrisome was precisely a lack of clear guidelines in in terms of one's bearings. It was a such a peculiar kind of fear. Some people insisted on drinking only mineral water in order to free those who were making soup or coffee with tap water from the responsibilities of the situation. Others said that certain books shouldn't be read or that certain types of music shouldn't be listened to. When a particular author published his first book of short stories, the publisher requested that he review the text and remove all of the dirty words." Removing the dirty words would be synonymous with not not telling and with negating history. Each of the stories set down in this text repudiates negation. Each says no to forgetting.

Perhaps the reader will find that these two voices and ways of creating memory divulge a similarity, that of the silenced women whose land, identity and language were torn away from them and that of the Jewish women who came to America in the nineteen twenties with the European migrations. Both groups coincide in their experience of silence and commencement and they help us rethink the omens and tasks of memory. A corollary exists between them; their common denominators are times of silence and seasons of utterance. These were also eras that coincided with military violence in certain countries, and these writings straightforwardly confirm the necessity of speech. Testimony discloses evidence of horror, of the trauma of physical and moral torture and of indifference. But it also presents history and its documentation as an everyday, collective effort.

How is memory elaborated and maintained? It is precisely within the process of writing that memory is put together. Women devise memory through writing. Indigenous women reconstruct on cloth, and in so doing they compose and tie together their destinies. Women victims of the military dictatorship construct memory with leftover pieces of cloth and words: the raw materials of poverty. Memory transforms into the essence of that which is feminine. It is silent intertwining and weaving that narrate the stories by which women recover their identity. Writing does not necessarily have to be written. Every oral testimony, more than a venue of witness, implicates us. It involves us in experience of communities and in the secrets of people surrounded by the mist of "otherness." The indigenous community and rural women's groups participate in this sense of sharing and revealing the ideology which predominates, but they are also another kind of telling: words which play at transformation.

If women's writing has been closer to silence, whispering, and servant's rooms as Tamara Kamenzain proposes in *Texto Silencioso* (Silent Text), it follows that testimonial literature of the seventies and Jewish women writer's testimony share histories of land and immigration apart from that dialogue of women who, in a given historic moment, spontaneously and intuitively began to tell.

In a recent conversation Ana Maria Shua told me that her grandparents worked the land and wrote stories in the Province of Entre Ríos in Argentina. The discourse of rural women and Jewish writers takes place within both of these dimensions. Their writings have to do with roots and finding themselves. The stories fluctuate between love and its absence. They are songs and experiences, speculations about the past and ways to dwell in the present. because women's writing in and of itself is a chronicle of imagination and memory.

Since the nineteen seventies, the testimonial creation of women does more than accommodate itself to the process of writing and telling stories. To me it seems next to impossible to capture the testimony of these voices and classify them into different types of testimonies such as political, magical, feminine, or anthropological. Women's testimony is situated within an area as ambiguous as the fragmented lives of those who write while simultaneously preparing a little mole sauce or washing clothes that belong to other people. The oral testimony of these voices narrates and revives dialogue, along with the very scenario of orality itself, without any desire to fictionalize or market it. This is a sacred, *mestiza* voice. It is a voice that truly seduces because it has an almost secret part to it, one which is impossible to categorize or connect. The emo-

tion with which the testimony is narrated and the way the dialogue is orga-
nized are acts that inspire, as is the secret story whispered in the ear. Perhaps
that is what is being told. And in the process of removing masks, a very basic
schism is created between the empty text where these voices reside and the
text which now imposes its presence and revokes absence.

The testimonies of ordinary women come together under the correlative of
sacred ritual, the presence of orality and the ritual of the one who listens, be
that in written form or through the process of compiling. We must keep in
mind that there are no secrets or communion without the existence of another
person to whom the secret can be told. There is no story unless a testimony is
offered up and then placed within a reality which almost intuitively prepares
to listen to that story and to love it.

The relevancy of these testimonies is their presence, which dates back thou-
sands of years and attempts to write oral tradition, eventually reshaping the
language of all women. Why all the effort to incorporate these women into
written discourse when oral discourse has been the major idiom of women?
To answer this complicated question, one must ponder on those marketing
systems which try to place a value on that obsessive search to to tell a story
again and again. Perhaps it would be the illusion of the compiler to grant only
to the written word the origin of that which is sacred.

After the compiling and writing of these testimonial texts, will there be a
new ideology? Will it be necessary to meditate about the intimate and personal
relationship between the academician who compiles the story and the woman
who is telling it? The individual who goes about the task of compiling will
have to learn to approach the regions of the divine, the sacred, and ritual. And
from that same ritual, he or she will create a new ritual that is rooted in lan-
guage and dialogue located between orality and writing.

Translated by Diane Russell-Pineda

TALKING ABOUT CULTURE:
CHILE AND THE UNITED STATES

Seen on a map, my country, Chile, looks like a long, narrow strip of land. Renowned historian Benjamin Subercaseux described Chile as "a crazy geography." Poet Pablo Neruda sang of its snowy Andean peaks as the petals of a rose; the poet Gabriela Mistral noted in her conversations and writings that Chileans lived locked in between the mountains and the sea, and that, although they were insular and reserved, they were at the same time friendly and generous.

Is it geography—the colorful spaces of mountains and valleys—that defines a national identity? How does one speak of her nation? How does one paint a landscape of identity? What does it mean to have faith in one's homeland?

The geography of Chile with its intense greens and its devouring mountains has always been an obsession for its inhabitants. We have had to create the language with which to describe a landscape that shrinks us into small specks of human life. Chile incites us to invent a way of speaking and a way of pulsating before its overpowering geography.

We Chileans are characterized by a humility similar to that of Third World people or of people far removed from contact with other nations. Nevertheless, this spectacular geography often makes us a united, hospitable nation. It is not unusual for Chileans to offer their homes to foreigners, to friends of friends, to the homeless, to the vulnerable, and to the *allegados*.

The concept of the *allegado*—a close friend or close relative, from *allegar*, to bring near or unite—is common in Chile and in the social imagination of its inhabitants. The *allegado* is a person, be it a relative or a complete stranger, who is welcomed into the home of another, sharing the abundance or the scarcity, receiving food and shelter as proof of the enduring fact that he/she is not, and should not be, alone.

These reflections about my country make me think about the United States, a country in which I have lived for many years but in which I have not felt completely at home. The concept of the *allegado* is inconceivable in this excessively individualistic, private, alienating culture where contact with other human beings is rare. North Americans are raised with a strong sense of personal independence. They are accustomed to their children working at an early age and leaving home when quite young. And although they may return home when their finances are precarious, they don't do it to be with their family. In fact, it would seem that outward signs of affection are more acceptable in this country when directed toward animals than toward fellow human beings.

The *allegado* has no place in this pragmatic Anglo-Saxon society, so blindly obedient to the ties and indoctrination of its own ideology. It is frightening that in one of the most powerful countries of the Western world, the number of homeless or street people is increasing at an alarming rate. Why is there no one to open a door to them? Who offers them a helping hand? Why aren't they fed at night? Where are the families of the homeless? And where are the citizens who observe this rising flood of people, so depersonalized and alone?

In Latin America the individual takes an active position when faced with the silence and indifference of a government that doesn't care for the homeless. Paradoxically, the Latin American citizen is active without relying on the official networks of the government. It is the individual, not an indifferent system, who opens the doors for the helpless. In the United States, on the other hand, where it is assumed that the individual is self-governing, the citizen actually allies him/herself closely with an oppressive government through passivity and indifference in the area of social responsibility.

The Latin American, unlike many North Americans, doesn't trust the prevailing systems of order or government. Citizens realize that they must control their own lives, that they cannot wait for the decrees of the government. I find it impossible to imagine a Latin American government setting up shelters for the homeless, just as I cannot imagine a Latin American refusing to help a beggar. I also find it difficult to comprehend how so many people in the United States can look at the homeless with indifference simply because they do not fit into the operant system of domination.

The terms "mercy" and "compassion" are significant in Latin American society. We are overwhelmingly catholic in spite of being Jewish, Protestant, and Moslem. We are catholic in the Mediterranean sense of the word: we prefer to be cheerful, we are drawn to the sun, to the light, to the here and now, to physical contact with others, to the touch, to the kiss. We are caring and compassionate with children and tender with the elderly, whom we care for in our homes.

The concept of morality in Chile and the rest of Latin America does not reside in a morality camouflaged by a false sexual modesty.It is a morality based on compassion and the generous *abrazo*, the hug. For example, it wasn't unusual during the monstrous, dark days of the dictatorship for the police to play soccer with the students or for supporters of the regime to hide the adversary in their homes because, after all, they were human beings too, fellow Chileans.

"Morality" and "compassion" are spoken of in the United States also. The words of George Bush during his first presidential campaign indicated that the United States would be a beacon, a thousand points of light for other countries to follow, that this country would be generous with weak nations. Is that why, during the Persian Gulf War, Iraqi women and children were killed to defend a tyrannical, autocratic ruler who was obviously rich in oil? And why the Israeli people had to wear gas masks, making them remember the recent genocide carried out against them? Where was Bush during the dismemberment of Yugoslavia?

North American politics in recent decades coincides to a great extent with a monstrous degeneration in the fabric of society and its morality toward "the other." The words "values" and "morals" are repeated often while, at the same time, ultrareactionary groups speak out against abortion, and black babies and black adolescents die. Few families are willing to adopt black or dark-skinned children.

If there is anything that characterizes the decade of the Republican regime, it is the lack of compassion for the underprivileged, for those without a voice, for women and children. In this respect, the Republican government is parallel in many ways to the fascist Chilean system that increased the poverty of women, of the young and the poor, and rewarded with privileges those who supported the regime.

Compassion, a way of living, of eating, of writing, of loving—these are all reflections of a people and of their country. In my country there is as great a love of poetry as there is of food; young and old alike are dedicated to the lyrical art. They are familiar with the masters of verse—Neruda, Mistral, Parra—but they are also daring and independent. They like to write and recite poetry, play the guitar, and drink with friends. In Chile, as in other Latin American countries, the spirit of community extends from the small everyday events to the major historical events. People still have time to get together for a cup of coffee or to share a glass of red wine in the afternoon.

In the United States time is fragmentary: there is a time for work, a time for pleasure, and a time for drinking. In such a system there is little opportunity to gather together to share work, to share a drink, to share love and affection. Communal activities for Latin Americans form part of daily life; they aren't relegated to group meetings at church or to the infinite number of singles' clubs whose members feel ever more solitary, more impoverished in soul and body.

Life in the United States consists of an agitated sigh, a flight in which the day passes by without time for pleasantries, without time to think or read a poem, to sketch or write a letter. Life drives the human being who, in turn, confused and frustrated, inhabits the days without really living them.

In other areas of the world where the Mediterranean culture prevails, such as the south of France or southern Spain, the ways of living and loving are similar to those of the southern part of the American hemisphere. In Provence one can enjoy to the fullest a sunny day, the bright blue windows, a glass of *vin rouge* at noon; so, too, in far away Chile the world stops at lunchtime, friends greet each other with a pat on the back, touch one another, and part with two or three kisses on the cheek.

In the United States touching is an anomaly. People seldom shake hands upon meeting a stranger or even a friend. The pleasure of touching and of getting acquainted in this society of technocrats and gurus is reduced to the insincere rituals of "how to live." This artificial "how to" approach creates, I believe, an absence of intimacy since real intimacy is not found in sexual liberty, but rather in the capacity to enter into a true communion with "the other," of being able to caress in moments of loneliness or to offer a bed or a parcel of food in a moment of need.

The fear of poetry does not exist in Latin American societies. In the United States, however, poetry tends to be an invisible activity or profession, tied to academia, and separate from the rest of society. Here, for example, only poets attend poetry readings, an ancient art form that is becoming increasingly more fragmented and removed from community life. It is tragic that the purest and most essential form of language is becoming part of the invisible, absent fabric of culture. Perhaps that is why politicians can so easily turn words into traps, lies, banalities. It seems that the more the North American desires privacy, the more he/she is incapable of feeling, of sharing, of participating in an ongoing dialogue. The North American, by attempting always to take refuge in him/herself, takes refuge in no place. He/she no longer has a place or a connection with others and desperately seeks to belong. The lonely person resorts, then, to organized belonging: clubs for singles, clubs for homosexuals, clubs for heterosexuals, for mothers with children, for mothers without children, and so on.

The *allegado,* on the other hand, is absorbed into the home or the shack of his/her real or adopted family. In Latin America one isn't afraid to touch the heart of another for a day, for a night, for a lifetime, and to make a true cult of friendship. The free pleasures of good conversation, of drinking together, and of saying good-bye with a kiss on both cheeks still exist. Perhaps this is why the concept of the *allegado* has no room in North American society, just as the concept of privacy isn't found in our society. One has to wonder who lives more happily—or who really lives at all.

Translated by Margaret Stanton

THE DISENCHANTED
GENERATION

In Chile my generation, born between 1950 and 1955, is called the "disenchanted generation." Shrouded in violence, we were the children of war. We witnessed buses being set on fire and older women being dragged away by their shining, long hair. The generation closest to us in age, those born in the 1960s and 1970s, couldn't understand us. We sat enraptured in cafes and talked about the beauty of the sky and earth for hours on end. The looked at us suspiciously. We, "the disenchanted," learned not to confide in them; they, "the invisible generation," had grown up under a legacy of violence and terror and, yet, it is they who are responsible for the re-vision and reconstruction of a dismembered society, polarized and dispirited by its own history. They were the ones who continued hearing the echoed voices of the disappeared. We *were* the disappeared.

For those of us Chileans who survived, the disenchanted and the invisible, just walking through our neighborhoods and smelling familiar scents wafting from shops and street corners is pleasurable. It's also gratifying to know that certain avenues covered with smog still smell of gardenias. It is still possible to turn a corner, go left, and continue straight until you reach the mountains, and to see our grandparents watching their television sets as though nothing happened. But what did happen?

Our social struggle coincided with the most politically repressive years in the Southern Cone. We contributed the word "disappeared" to the vernacular of horror, and this word is now common in everyday conversations. Confused and deluded, we asked about our lost ones, those who went nameless to a potter's field. And, now, after twenty years of terror, we ask not for justice or revenge but just for truth. My disenchanted generation talks about democracy, but we haven't asked if democracy will erase the footprints, the scars of an insane past where certain nations–among them Argentina, the most cultivated of the Southern Cone–succumbed to a Nazi paranoia. Would it be possible to compromise and rationalize with these military groups who in search of the so-called national security, roamed desperately in the night to kidnap people who might have been, or seemed to be, subversive because they liked to wear jeans or read Marx?

How do we forge reconciliation with those whose ideology consisted only of arbitrary arrests and in the most barbaric ceremony among human beings: torture. Perhaps only those who survived the torture sessions will one day be able to tell us and help us to imagine, if only for a second, the legacy for the disenchanted generation and the invisible generation: the legacy of horror.

For those who survived, who suffered incarceration because of their ideals, who were beaten over and over again in order that they reveal other names or the bus stop of their friends, we must ask if these "dirty wars" have had any effect on or have provoked a change in the citizens of the Southern Cone. For Jacobo Timmerman the answer is no. In a recent interview, Timmerman says: "I don't think the 'dirty war' had any effect at all on Argentines. What really did produce an impact was the economic and political structure organized by Peron in the '40s. That is our present reality. Before 1983, Argentines had no interest whatsoever in human rights and very few care about them now.

"Let me tell you about my experience. I am searching for a small apartment here in Buenos Aires, because now I live in Punta del Este. I want a place where I can live with my wife and children, but three times we have been turned down by owners who say they can't rent to us because they don't want trouble."

The observation made by Jacobo Timmerman in neighboring Argentina is applicable to Chile. Wouldn't it be easier to avoid the collective memory of a collective crime? Is it easier to know, without admitting it, that torturers occupy our cities, that they are seen in cafés and restaurants or taking their children to school?

My disenchanted generation reads articles about the Human Rights Commission, the famous Rettig Report that is sold at kiosks in our Chilean cities, the same kind of report that was sold in Argentina bearing thousands and thousands of names, dates and times referring to those who were captured and were never heard from again. The majority of the subversives were between the ages of sixteen and twenty. If they were alive they would be my age with families, houses, jobs, in short, decent lives. They didn't want war. Some believed passionately in social change, in the building of schools and health clinics, but, ah yes, these subversive goals could have destroyed the national security.

Years ago in Argentina, Fernando Gonzalez wrote a moving piece about his generation, known as "the invisible generation" in his country, in which he stated, "When the military took power in Argentina, everything was transformed into something surreal and deadly. Our reality was full of phantoms and ghoulish characters. We had an aging general, Juan Peron; his third wife, a cabaret singer...and along with her, José Lopez Rega, who specialized in the occult..."

Gabriel Garcia Marquez, with reason, said in his Nobel speech that we Latin Americans shouldn't demand much from our imagination because the horrors which beset us in our daily life are ominous enough.

But now I ask: how should we live? We are not only a disenchanted generation, but also a dispersed generation. Exiled in North America, Europe, in other Latin American countries, we try to ensure that our children speak Spanish, that they enjoy our Sunday customs: going to lunch with parents and relatives, going to the movies, having leisurely conversations in cafés. Those who live in exile within their country desperately try to survive; some succeed by means of memory. They support human rights groups, they assist forensic experts who unearth the remains of those who disappeared, they attend their funerals, they bear testimony to the deaths of others. The next generation prefers silence, discretion and peace. They will not admit that the respectable colony Dignidad, in the south of Chile, was a refuge for Nazis and torture camps. Likewise, Argentines deny that there were approximately 340 clandestine concentration camps throughout their country—camps occupied by suspicious, bearded students, jean-clad women, children, pregnant girls, all of whom were "dangerous to the national security."

I dream constantly about my return to Chile after the euphoria and triumphs of President Alwyn, after the voluminous Rettig Report, similar to the

Nunca Mas document published in Buenos Aires. But upon my return I am even more terrified. Before, when my diminutive presence weighed down by poetry books was suspicious, my enemies were visible. Now my enemies are invisible and crafty. We are carrying pain, fear, terror. It is almost impossible for us to imagine that the children who were abducted while buying bread are still missing. The most fortunate are named in the Rettig Report. But is a name in a controversial publication, a publication still repudiated by its citizens and by the still-intact military apparatus, sufficient vindication for a death?

How does one survive where justice and truth are still threatening to a population awakening from insomnia and horror? How does one become reconciled to an older generation that feigns ignorance? Would it be possible not to know what was happening when the nights offered scenes of phantoms arbitrarily shooting at one another, when the curfews made us tremble? It was impossible not to know when Jews awaited trains during another war and other deaths in European plazas. I imagine returning to my country, crossing the Andes, so austere in their silence. But I also imagine myself arriving at a country where no family members exist; they are either exiled or dead of natural causes or of heartbreak. I don't know if I should first visit the living or go to the cemetery to acknowledge my dead. I imagine returning and talking to friends who are desperately trying to put their lives back together. They say that it is still possible to walk the streets of Santiago and inhale the fragrance of the gardenias and bougainvilea, and it is even possible to remember when we were innocent and to let ourselves be scared just for fun and to talk to friendly police.

The illusion is a contrast to the reality: a scene of poverty, juvenile prostitution, and dispirited beggars. There they are, with the repressive apparatus of the State still operating, as is General Pinochet, head of the armed forces for life. The clandestine cases of torture remain hidden, but if we get close to them we will hear certain screams, certain pleas. I think the dead demand truth more than justice. They don't ask for vengeance or retribution. Let us fearlessly ask for the truth, because only then will genuine reconciliation occur. Our lives, rooted in the past, will finally reach toward the future.

And what of the women, so many women who for so many years defied an ominous silence? Those who dared to be pushed off grand boulevards with their posters: 'Where are they?" and 'We love them with our life." Those women–mothers, grandmothers, granddaughters and sisters–form our collective memory, one single hug, one lonely white handkerchief opening like a cupola toward the horizon. It is precisely those women to whom we owe what we vaguely call our conscience. Women throughout Latin America challenged the ruling authoritarianism in Montevideo, Buenos Aires and Santiago. They crossed Central America, they dared to go out on the streets, leave their homes, their patios, their markets. I see them unified in an immense, inimitable sadness over the loss of their children; I see them railing, raising photographs of a disappeared son or grandson. We must never forget that in many countries two generations are completely lost: parents and children born in captivity and adopted illegally by their captors.

The movements of women in Latin America will be remembered as some of the most visible and central events of our political history because they began to define the one thousand ways and manners of playing politics, a politics based on collective spectacle, in firmly standing in immense plazas calling out to the lost, drawing silhouettes without faces on the pavement, making sure that the disappeared are remembered. And they sewed tapestries of truth, the famous *arpilleras* that tell the stories of an ambushed country.

I imagine another homecoming: I call all of the women who during these years formed an essential part of my country, those who told me their life stories and those who comprehended that the pain of another is authentic. They remain without answers about the destiny of their loved ones, without truth or justice. Some of the most active have died, such as our beloved Irma Muller, marvelous singing *arpillerista,* a constant fountain of life. And we remember her and understand and accept, perhaps for the first time, that death is the only possible and true alternative to weariness. Let us not forget their songs, their distraught faces, their pain as they crossed the thresholds of their empty homes, their lonely kitchens.

We are the disenchanted generation. Nevertheless we are nostalgic when we hear certain revolutionary songs of the '70s being sung in cafés. We have children now. We work to educate them; we must survive. Yet we try to overcome the real legacies of the dictatorships: the lack of mutual trust; the fear of building, revising and rethinking ways of being. We are the disenchanted generation, but yet we sing and hope that this time our memory will not be false or ambiguous, that it instead will be healing and daring, like the hands of our children, open hands that have not been dirtied with blood. Innocent and reaching hands. Perhaps they will be the Enchanted Generation.

Translated by Lori M. Carlson

DEMOCRACY
FOR A GHOST NATION

During seventeen monstrous years of dictatorship, 1973-1988, I would travel to my native Chile. I longed to see the faces of the people, to take in the aroma of peaches and summer, to behold from the heights and the distance the implacable Andes. Touching down on the Chilean soil implied an endless number of consequences, such as possible detention by the national police due to my suspicious activities, which consisted of writing poetry against the dictatorship—poems with the voices of the disappeared—and speaking atNorth American universities of the Chilean *arpilleras*, political tapestries sewn from scraps by women relatives of the disappeared. In these tapestries, a political history was told, a history plagued by horror, hunger, fear.

In January of 1992, I return to my country, even though every return means a clash, a confrontation, a second meeting with my generation, a lucid and dynamic generation, always willing to talk, open to dialogue. More than anything, we are a generation schooled in political and ideological matters. That's why we disappeared into the prisons and torture chambers and only exiguous memory managed to save us.

Summer in the Southern Cone is luminous and diaphanous. The Andes are visible from afar and it seems as if there is a blizzard of air. My country is beautiful and grieving and yet it is now ours. Or is it? The secret police no longer inhabit the small Pudahuel Airport. We all enter happily, as before. We embrace as before, and the fear of the unexpected seems unwarranted. But we should ask ourselves: Are we as before?

The Chilean military dictatorship murdered our youth. They built gargantu-
an cement monuments, such as the one known as the White Elephant, the
Chilean Congress in Valparaiso, an enormous building of immense rooms
erected by Pinochet. This Chilean dictator destroyed our political life, our
desire to talk about ideologies, ethical and moral values. The Pinochet dicta-
torship muzzled us and, paradoxically, continues to silence us in the new
democratic times.

It seems odd to listen to people of my generation speak of the ever present
and never resolved problem of human rights: to speak about the fact that the
repressive military apparatus is intact is a forbidden subject. The famous
Rettig report, created by the commission appointed in 1990 by President
Alwyn to document human rights violations, now remains forgotten, in
silence. Nobody speaks about anything in today's Chile. Democracy has trans-
formed us into a solitary, silent people that still shudder, kept busy only by
our daily chores. To speak of human rights or testimonial literature is now out
of style, an issue of the past. To speak of folklore and popular culture is also
to speak of unpleasant subjects. So what do we speak of–and why?

My generation was one that fought side by side with Salvador Allende to
bring about real social and ideological change. Many gave their lives for the
dream of a fair and just society. And because we fought the dictatorship, our
generation was silenced and mutilated.

The hopeful effervescence of the final years of the dictatorship and the
democratic triumph of President Alwyn have been left behind in the collective
memory. The problem of the disappeared and their surviving families also
becomes a distasteful topic of conversation at social gatherings. A great
silence, thick and hazy, envelops us.

I am in Chile in 1992 and I realize, overcome with nostalgia and a touch of
naive romanticism, that during the years of the dictatorship we were more
audacious, intrepid and less silent. We should ask ourselves why we are now
so distant from our own selves and why we are so solitary in the midst of this
democratic process which promised historic reforms of great significance.

I believe that we should not blame anyone, least of all the current president
who must of necessity choose the path of reconciliation and caution because
he must still contend with the dictator who continues to control the nation's
political life.

The fascist dictatorship left us a legacy of internalized fear and fatigue. We are exhausted after seventeen years of dread and horror; we are tired of political promises and of words such as stability, order and justice. My generation now prefers the withdrawn life, home and security, rather than revolutionary nostalgia. Part of this is due to maturity, but part is due to the legacy of an offensive manipulative dictatorship.

It is important for the Western democracies to understand that the legacy of a dictatorship is sinister, profound, leaving permanent scars. There still exists in the minds of young parents the fear that the military power might revive in our country. There still exists the fear that during the night there will be a knock on the door to take us away because we are innocent youths with political beliefs and values. The Chilean dictatorship never tolerated political dialogue nor dissident ideas. It did not allow the young to make history, and this legacy has scarred us. Life in Chile now transpires in silence, the controversial political topics have been put on the back shelves, assigned to oblivion, and the worst thing is that we have not yet understood what happened to us, how fear transformed us, and what we have to do to heal ourselves. The only strong voice of opposition and resistance that is now heard in my country comes from the Association of the Detained-Disappeared. The members fight with the same obstinacy and strength of the past seventeen years. They still march by the gates of Congress and on the squares carrying photographs of their loved ones: they are a living presence of a silenced memory.

During my stay in Chile, I always visit the offices of the Association and they fill me in about what is happening in the country, not only ideologically and politically, but also on the deeper level: at the level of human ethics. The relatives of the disappeared, along with the majority of Chilean citizens, want reconciliation, but reconciliation consists of many different nuances. The reconciliation for the relatives is not forgetfulness or amnesty but rather public recognition that the military dictatorship acted illegally and clandestinely, that they kidnapped, tortured and murdered human beings who had not been found guilty in any trial. The relatives do not seek revenge or death in retribution. They do ask that the perpetrators be tried by civilian courts and jailed if found guilty for the crimes they committed. It is perplexing to think that to date in the countries of the Southern Cone no military official is now in prison. The historic trials under Alfonsín have been forgotten.

Conversation with the relatives is active and profound. I feel that I am finally in that Chile of yesteryear where discussion, political expression, and open debate were our trademarks. But political dialogue should not exist only during the years of the dictatorship.

I take leave of my friends, of Carmen, of Violeta, with that embrace that promises a return, that promises that we will not forget each other, because the greatest fear of the victims of state terrorism and their relatives is the silence of complicity.

From a distance and from voluntary exile, I write about my country. Through my absence I invent myself, and I imagine a politically active Chile, a Chile that thinks for itself and creates its own awareness. I hope these wishes of utopia invented in the cloister of a North American university are not only a chimera. I have a deep conviction that my country will again look at itself in the depths of its fear and horror and will have the awareness and wisdom to accept the reflection from its broken and bloody mirror, a mirror which arises and reconstructs itself, transparent and clear. "History," Salvador Allende stated in his inaugural speech, "is created by nations. Our history in this democratic process is about to be created. We will no longer be a ghost nation but rather a nation of light and life."

Translated by Paula M. Vega

CITIES OF LIFE,
CITIES OF CHANGE

Latin American cities used to possess an immediate sexuality, an eroticism of power reflected by the men—enemies of silence and lifelong partners of wine—who traveled the endless voyages of the night. They populated the long Latin American evening, while women were obliged to remain reclusive and silent. Women were the guardians, the ones who appeared only for farewell ceremonies, the ones who asked for silence and love when they had to wash the dead or save the living.

With the military dictatorships of the 1970s, the faces of the cities changed. The plazas where men used to gather were filled with the ghosts of the disappeared and the fear of further violence. Drunk with terror, Latin Americans were left with the tortured, dead bodies that appeared in the cities, in the doorways of bars, along the riverbanks, or in their own neighborhoods.

As the cities filled with bodie, and the odor of ashes invaded the spaces once inhabited by moss and leafy trees, the women went out into the streets, gathered and cleaned the bodies, and buried their loved ones with the dignity of the innocent. In this way, the cities became populated by hidden women who began to shout that they did not want any more of this sinister cult of death, that they were tired of the swords, the masculine violence, and the battles occurring every minute of the day and night.

Latin American cities that had been dominated by authoritarianism were slowly taken over by women. The first associations of the detained and disappeared in Chile, Argentina, and El Salvador were born from the perseverance of women.[1] They were the ones to protest and to search the prisons and the courts for their loved ones, sinisterly called "the disappeared." They challenged the dictatorships as mothers, but in a way that went beyond their bio-logical roles to encompass a celebration and affirmation of human life and the negation of torture and death.

Movements such as the Mothers of the Plaza de Mayo were born from these associations, again filling the cities with women's faces. These groups spon-sored ceremonies in a number of cities demanding the return of the disap-peared. For example, in Buenos Aires, women began to gather in the Plaza de Mayo, where children still play and grandmothers knit soft warm sweaters for future winters. Since 1976, groups of women have met in the plaza to circle one of the most public and political spots in the city: the place where men from Juan Peron to General Videla presented the "official"—that is, mascu-line—story. These leaders decided who would die, who would live, who would be tortured with cattle prods.

Then the women arrived, and they literally began to take over the city. At first, there were only fourteen mothers; now there are hundreds. The fourteen heads covered with kerchiefs and the placards bearing photographs of the missing multiplied, and the plaza was filled with kerchiefs, flowers, and women greeting each other. Every Thursday they march around the obelisk. a phallic symbol that they transformed into something feminine. The Mothers took over the same plaza that was previously the site of speeches that addressed only the themes of war and victory.

The plaza became a center for commemorating the missing. The women carried out events that they called "art actions" and "actions for life." They covered the city's trees with enormous photographs of the missing, their eyes asking not to be forgotten. They also sponsored "marches for resistance," where the Mothers circled the Plaza de Mayo for twenty-four consecutive hours. Through the struggle for truth and justice, the great city of Buenos Aires experienced a unique metamorphosis, despite existing on the border between life and death.

From Argentina, where the Mothers of the Plaza de Mayo were often called crazy for having dared to ask where their children were and why they were taken, we cross the enormous snowy mountain peaks to reach Chile. Santiago is another great city populated by women who continually sponsor actions for life in the streets and are pursued by military officers and their attack dogs. Also on Thursdays, they march around the former tribunals of justice and, as their Argentine neighbors, carry photographs of their missing children strapped to their chests.

The protests of Chilean women won international fame because they feminized the city, utilizing techniques traditionally associated with domesticity. The first event of this type that occurred in the city had to do with pots and pans. The phenomenon of the empty pots took place during 1972 and 1973 when women demanded the resignation of the president, Salvador Allende.

During that period, women gathered at a certain time and paraded throughout the city, banging casserole dishes to protest the scarcity of food. The ceremony of the empty pots filled the great city of Santiago with strange and frightening sounds. In reality, there was no scarcity; food was being hoarded by members of the CIA and the Chilean oligarchy with the purpose of destabilizing the country's economy to create chaos. This course of action ended in the defeat and assassination of Dr. Allende.

Again, women took over a city, creating a new, alternative political culture. But the women who complained about their empty pots were from the upperclass neighborhoods, the ones who went onto their gilded balconies with their poor maids to demand the end of a socialist government.

Almost fifteen years later, the protests have taken on a different rhetoric. Women from the poor neighborhoods march through the city beating tin cans and pots, women who really do not have anything to eat. Their actions represent the noisy sounds of hunger asking for the justice of a meal.

Other groups of marginal women, the inhabitants of shantytowns on the outskirts of Santiago, have invented new strategies to survive, to combat hunger and cold. A group of brave women organized the country's first Association of the Detained/Disappeared in 1974 under the protection of the Vicaria de la Solidaridad, a human rights organization linked to the Catholic church. In the middle of the immense city, seemingly wealthy and orderly, the women of the shantytowns organized to find their missing children.

In addition to forming this organization, the mothers of the disappeared began to make *arpilleras,* small collages formed from scraps, rags, and pieces of material that had been thrown away and forgotten.[2] These wounded and robbed women began to meet in the middle of the dehumanized city to construct the story of their lives with these pieces of cloth. Each tapestry, anonymously made, reflects a life that has been destroyed and violated by the military regime, as well as the possibility of a better future.

All of the abysmal conditions of the city such as the lack of water, schools, and medical attention are described in these *arpilleras,* which speak with the innocence of children but which have the ability to accuse, denounce, and expose to the world the horrors of a fascist state.

These *arpilleras* are not shown within the city; the few exhibitions that have been attempted have been negatively received and have ended with violence and repression against the participants. Nevertheless, the city appears in the artistic work of each *arpillerista.* Each woman in the workshops insists on depicting the city accurately, its neighborhoods, and its trees, which at times bear on their trunks the names of the disappeared and the time they disappeared.

The city has never been represented with such honesty and truth and in such a female form. Certain metaphors and objects are brought to the cloth, especially the Andes mountains, which surround the city and, at night, give it an aura of hope. The mountains allow people to dream of a land full of possibilities and a new freedom.

Within the city, another important phenomenon, the "communal pots," appears with great regularity. Without the support of an outside agency, the women spontaneously organized communal kitchens to help combat poverty. In each outlying section a neighborhood kitchen with common pots is formed where, once a day, children can obtain food to be able to survive the long day ahead of them. The *arpilleras* tell of the communal pots and of the solidarity that is found over a shared plate of food. The women transform the harsh city into a community, into a place where it is possible to survive and to defeat hunger.

The actions of the *arpilleristas* and of the women who transform the plazas into centers of political and ethical protest have managed to humanize cities full of walls, both imaginary and actual, and to reclaim their spaces. From the Plaza de Mayo in Buenos Aires to the center of San Salvador, women have begun to invent strategies to defy fear. They do it through peaceful means while constructing a clearly female symbolism with white kerchiefs and unclenched hands, which mean: our hands are clean; we haven't killed or tortured anyone.

The male-dominated Latin American culture that confined women to enclosed spaces, to the back alleys of history where they were treated as if they were invisible, has been transformed, and the presence of women has become more and more powerful and defiant. Women have subverted and transformed the roles that the fascist state assigned to them: the dictatorship searched for women to play the role of mothers serving the homeland, but instead, women began to search for their dead children whom the same homeland took away.

Women march throughout the city carrying signs that say "No more because we are more." They create "art actions" where women from different parts of the city march and gather in a central spot each holding a colorful ribbon, making it possible to dream of escape from the labyrinth of death by forging an invincible link of human life. In this way, these Ariadne[3] have truly created a new, free city using a female imagery born from repression.

Translated by Janice Molloy

WOMEN, POLITICS, AND SOCIETY IN CHILE

The spatial layout of Latin American cities has a strong relation to gender. Since the colonial period, women tended to be confined to their homes and interior patios, only leaving their enclosed spaces accompanied by others to shop. Plazas, historical monuments, and streets were, in general, forbidden places for them. Yet, some women began to leave their gendered space in the twentieth century to organize on behalf of their own interests. The decade of the 1970s marked the end of so-called male and female territories; women's political activity was transformed in response to the policies and practices of their countries' authoritarian regimes.

THE EMERGENCE OF WOMEN'S MOVEMENTS

Before discussing the various Chilean women's movements, some light should be shed on the economic and political climate that served as a backdrop to them. From the Industrial Revolution to Salvador Allende's presidency in 1971, Chile had a democratic government and an economic system of liberal capitalism similar to those of other developing countries of the region, namely, Argentina and Uruguay. Also during this time, Chile's mineral wealth was increasingly discovered and expropriated, and the economy flourished. Few records or documents exist about Chilean women's early political activity during these years. As early as 1913, however, miners' wives organized the Bellen de Zaraga Center in the northern mining regions of Chile to protest employee exploitation and human rights violations. A variety of women's groups also emerged in the 1900s to work for women's education. Among the women who spearheaded this drive were two teachers, Amanda Labarca and Gabriela Mistral. They formed reading groups, such as the Women's Reading Circle, to encourage intellectual inquiry, and they gave many Chilean women their first educational experience .

In 1919, the year the Women's Reading Circle was established, feminists also discussed women's position in the National Council of Women, a nationally organized women's group. There, activists such as Inez Echeveria addressed the need for women's and children's education. These two groups gave birth to a feminist initiative which became, in 1922, a major campaign to gain civil and political rights for women, that is, the incorporation of women into society as full citizens and as the framers of their own political, civil, and judicial identity.

Also in 1919, the President was petitioned to franchise women and the Chilean Women's Party was established. The Party called for reform of legislation concerning women, suffrage and civil rights for women, improvement of conditions for women and children, guidance for and protection of children and pregnant women, and women's right to be independent and autonomous in all political and religious groups.

Like their foremothers, members of the Chilean Women's Party emphasized the importance of education for women. In their view, emancipation was possible only when women understood how prevailing ideologies and norms simultaneously glorified women by placing them on a pedestal as wives and mothers and limited women by confining them to the domestic sphere. The Party created centers to raise women's awareness of their exploitation in the work place, thereby hoping to incorporate working women into the struggle for reform.

Unfortunately, the Chilean Women's Party was not completely successful in its efforts, although the reasons for its failure are obscure. The Party's failure possibly resulted from its lack of organization and the problems it encountered in gaining a varied base of support; the group was made up exclusively of upper-class women and was unable to attract a wide range of members. Julieta Kirkwood, author of *Ser mujer política en Chile* (To Be a Political Woman in Chile) and others argue, however, that the Chilean Women's Party was undermined by its essentialist view of women. While Party members considered all women to have special powers that made them "superior" beings and, therefore, all equal, they failed to incorporate lower-class women into the Party ranks.

In 1931, women were granted the right to vote in municipal elections, and the years that followed saw the emergence of a number of women's organizations. Two groups were established in 1936: The Movement for the Emancipation of Chilean Women and Feminine Action, a group associated with the Chilean Women's Party. Their goals were conservative, concerned mostly with traditional women's issues such as child care, health care, and maternity laws.

The Movement of Chilean Women (Movimiento de la Mujer Chilean/ MEMCH), a third and contrasting group also founded in 1936, drew its vision from the political left, and was consequently more politicized. In the view of the group's members, the problems of women could be resolved only by challenging both the material and ideological bases of women's subordination. Such a broadly defined program was extraordinary; it was relevant both to the bourgeoisie and the proletariat, and it called for women's suffrage as well as the diffusion of birth control methods to the poor. With respect to the latter, the MEMCH demonstrated great audacity, even temerity.

Although the differences between women's groups remained unresolved, they united on the issue of women's suffrage, and in 1949 women achieved the right to vote in national elections. Once this goal was achieved, however, women's organizations seemed to withdraw from the political arena.[1] Nevertheless, women began to vote regularly and to participate in political parties. Rather than developing their own political agendas, however, they identified with men's. They were not autonomous political actors.

Feminists who have studied Chilean women's political activity claim that their participation in politics increased during the 1950s and 1960s but was well concealed. Kirkwood, in *Ser mujer politica en Chile,* argues that women did not appear to be political actors because they had not yet developed a consciousness of their situation that transcended class; women identified only with members of their own class rather than with all women as a gender. Upper-class women, for example, viewed those in the lower class paternalistically, founding "people's closets" which offered charity to working-class women and women in marginal areas rather than uniting with them to work for a common goal.

During the 1950s and 1960s, the power of labor unions began to rise, due to the rise of the middle and lower classes under the liberal capitalist government. All sectors began to organize much more and this affected the women's groups. For the first time, labor unions were able to speak to workers' and women's groups.

To summarize, women began to organize in Chile in the early 1900s and their united efforts won women the right to vote in 1949. Nevertheless, women remained divided in Chile. The MEMCH developed a program to further the interests of working-class women, but these women remained marginal within the Party. Other groups, such as the Chilean Women's Party, held an essentialist view of women and considered all of them to be equal. Nevertheless, it failed to incorporate lower-class women into the Party's ranks. No group emerged during the 1950s and 1960s either to create a dialogue between women of different classes or to unite them in coordinated action. Contact between different women was embedded within a context of charity, with upper-class women the "generous givers" to the "grateful receivers" in the lower class.[2]

THE ALLENDE PERIOD: DEMOCRATIC SOCIALISM

In 1971, Salvador Allende and his Popular Union Party came to power. As a Marxist, Salvador Allende had a very different government agenda from what the country had previously known. He planned to vastly expand state control of industry and agriculture, as well as increase the living standards and political participation of the poor. Allende also raised the minimum wage and attempted to better public education. During Allende's regime, labor union organization increased due to Allende's political attention. The country's new climate, a direct result of changes incremented during the Allende administration, opened the political arena to women and gave them space in which to participate in it.

During the Allende years, people in the rural and marginal areas also had very little political participation. Groups for women, such as the Mother's Centers, were organized for the first time in rural areas, where they were especially needed. But, in general, rural women experienced the same difficulties as their working-class urban sisters. Middle class women still found it very hard to participate in political parties, for they lacked education concerning political systems and had no tradition of political participation. Women's political participation was a limited and isolated phenomenon, involving only upper-middle and upper class women in the cities.

Finally, Salvador Allende's fundamental political error was his constant iteration of traditional norms about women and their relationship to the domestic sphere. Women were viewed only as wives, mothers, daughters, and companions to male workers. Using the voice of the traditional bourgeois man, he stated that he valued them as mothers first and foremost:

> "When I speak of women I always think of the wife/mother. When I speak of women I refer to their function within the nuclear family. Children are the prolongation of the woman who is essentially born to be a mother."

The discourse of the progressive left focused on the nuclear family as the central axis of society, thereby perpetuating and reproducing a structure advanced by traditional right-wing groups. Salvador Allende and his Party changed only the terminology of the right-wing; rather than saying "the nuclear family," they spoke about "the proletarian family."

The voices of women were rarely heard during Allende's brief tenure. Nevertheless, Allende often alluded to the importance of women and their contributions to social and cultural change. Despite his rhetoric encouraging women's contributions, however, his brief presidency was notable for its lack of women in high positions. He nominated a woman for a position in his cabinet only after he had been in office two years. And none of the women who had fought so hard for the Socialist Party and the MAPU (Movement of Popular Actions) were appointed to leadership positions in the various agencies Allende initiated.

The women's projects proposed by Allende also were designed to confine women to traditional domestic roles. For example, he attempted to advance the interests of women by alleviating the daily chores of housework, by providing security to older women who could not work, and by establishing Mothers' Centers where sewing, knitting, and other such skills were taught. Undoubtedly, Allende wanted to incorporate women into his political agenda, but he was unable to overcome the traditional, male-oriented attitudes of

Chilean society which permeated his own thinking. Financial constraints, to be fair, also prevented him from initiating projects which might have benefited women. Allende's Popular Union Party also was unable to discard its own deeply-rooted chauvinism, despite its desire for change. The leftist press, which supported the party and Allende, perpetuated this chauvinism by casting women as sexual objects. For example, Mira Bambina demonstrates that the press constantly printed cartoons which depicted politically active women with bare legs and chests. The party's inability to alter its chauvinistic views may have hastened its downfall.

Women themselves may also have played a role in the undoing of Allende. Women of right-wing views protested against him near the end of his regime by banging pots together in public places. Many women felt great resentment towards Allende because they blamed him for the food shortages that occurred in 1972-73. The women's lack of enthusiasm manifested itself even earlier at the polls in 1971. Latin American women's tendency to assume the role of super-mothers helps explain this. In many Latin American countries women participated in political life by focusing on problems related to the domestic sphere; even women active in the Socialist party considered themselves appendages to men—companions of the active male participant. As mothers, then, the majority of Chilean women voted for conservative and traditional leaders.

These leaders were members of extreme right-wing parties who argued that the nation's values and security and the family's stability depended on a "moral force"—a "moral force" that women could find in their condition as women. They then used this rhetoric to mobilize women on behalf of their efforts to oust the alleged Communist government of Salvador Allende. Paradoxically, the women who were manipulated and organized in the struggle against Allende did not consider themselves among the ranks of those who were exploited because of their gender.

We will never know what a long-term socialist government like Allende's would have meant for women, since the regime fell tragically and dramatically in September 1973. Allende's attempt to abruptly transform Chile's political and social economic system ultimately caused unrest and instability since many from the upper classes opposed his reforms. Tensions mounted among political parties and between the various parties and the military and finally exploded in a military coup that ended Allende's term and his life. This extremely violent coup brought to power a general named Augusto Pinochet.

THE PINOCHET PERIOD: MILITARY AUTHORITARIANISM

Pinochet and his fellow members of the military junta intended to return to Chile its traditional, liberal, capitalist system, with an even stronger free market system. In reality the dictatorship imposed curfews and censorship and used severe repression and terror to quell any opposition. The regime claimed to stand against all communism and socialism, but in practice stood against democracy and civil liberties.

The regime's view on women was similar in some ways to that held by the Allende administration but differed in others. Although the new government was different from that of Allende, Augusto Pinochet also emphasized women's role as mother. The strategies devised to reinforce this role in Chilean society, however, were unique. Immediately after the 1973 coup, Pinochet created the National Bureau on Women, a unit designed to address women's problems such as hygiene and the care of children. In addition, he eliminated all but one of the few women's projects initiated by Allende during his term of office.

The Mothers' Centers were maintained, but they functioned as political units rather than as a training ground for women. There, women were indoctrinated in the Party line, that is, taught to guard family values and the social order. The authoritarian government of General Pinochet rejected the legitimacy of political organizations and women's groups. Its goal was not to mobilize women in the interest of political egalitarianism. Rather, the government's goal was to quell the voices of women and to suppress their political actions.

Chilean women, however, were not to be suppressed. In response to the political persecution of their loved ones, and with legal means to protest closed, women took to the streets—the area formerly prohibited to them. Under the banner of human rights, they demanded that the bodies of their disappeared and kidnapped relatives be returned, and that they be told the truth and the reasons why they had disappeared.

The first organization established in response to the plight of the disappeared was The Association of Relatives of the Detained and Disappeared (FEDEFAM). Formed in 1973 under the protection of the Catholic Archbishop of Santiago, the group was directly associated with the church, the champion of human rights in Chile. Few documents exist about FEDEFAM, but it is known that the organization included women of all classes and a range of ages who had lost loved ones and had united to find them.[3]

FEDEFAM was founded as a non-hierarchical organization, and remains such. Its members meet on a weekly basis at the Vicariate of Solidarity to discuss ways to pressure the government to meet their demands and to denounce the violations of human rights in Chile. In addition, the women of FEDEFAM organize protests on a regular basis. They hold candlelight vigils for the disappeared and, on one occasion, they chained themselves to the fence in front of the Congress building to publicize their demands for truth and justice.

The women of FEDEFAM also developed innovative strategies to transform a reality charged with fear and distrust. These new political strategies were based on a feminine creativity markedly different from the masculine norm. Among the best-known example of this creativity is the making of *arpilleras*— small tapestries in which women denounce Chile's political situation by illustrating events taking place in the country.

Using their sewing skills, women piece together bits of cloth into a whole that acquires a singular beauty. The *arpillera* makers manage to visually capture in their tapestries what words have been unable to express. Scenes of detention and torture and of hunger at community cafeterias appear throughout these tapestries. Yet each tapestry represents the unique vision and creation of the woman who made it.[4]

Although most of the *arpillera* makers, like most members of FEDEFAM, are economically and politically disadvantaged, to see them only as poor housewives looking for their missing children would be to oversimplify the creative and transformative process in which they are enmeshed. Organizations such as FEDEFAM give women, who were viewed only in relation to the domestic sphere, a new social identity as dissenting members of a community and a nation. This creativity and political expression endow women with a sense of power they had never previously experienced.

Between 1973 and 1980, FEDEFAM was the most visible organization within the closed authoritarian regime of Pinochet.[5] After 1980, however, Pinochet gradually began to lose power when the Chilean people tired of the high personal price they were paying for the booming economy that the general promised but never really delivered. His weakening position created a political opening for women to mobilize and organize for the improvement of living conditions, the study of women's condition, the politicization of women, and the return to democracy.[6]

Groups such as The Committee for the Defense of the Human Rights of Women (CODEM), Women of Chile (MUDECHI), and The Movement of Community Women (MOMUPO) were established in 1980, and 1981 saw the emergence of Women for Socialism and the feminist society,

FURIA (Women for Life) also was formed during these years; it functioned as a coordinator for the different groups, bringing them together and uniting them to protest the dictatorship. The Movement of Chilean Women (MEMCH), originally founded as a leftist organization in 1936 and re-established in 1983, also had this potential, but it was rejected by the multi-party front of women leaders trying to unite women of center and rightist views in their struggle to re-establish democracy in Chile. All of these groups originated in silence, in a Chile that was politically deserted and desperately searching for the means and possibilities of survival. They were born as alternative ways to create a new political forum, a re-establishment of the pluralistic, democratic society of the past. These movements had no solid political platform, but they did have a common goal: the end of the totalitarian regime.

The women who were members of these organizations developed a new awareness of their ability to act and alter the state political status quo. They met on a weekly basis to develop plans of action, and their struggle culminated in 1989 with the Chilean referendum. This referendum was about leadership in the country, and it was specified by Pinochet himself. After sixteen years of authoritarian rule, he gave the people the choice of continuing his dictatorship or starting a new democracy. Not surprisingly, the people overwhelmingly voted for democracy.

THE ALWYN PERIOD:

Numerous changes have been implemented since the referendum's victory in favor of Patricio Alwyn. The repression, terror and censorship of the Pinochet dictatorship is being eradicated, and Chile has returned to its old tradition of democracy. The women's groups of the country can once again enjoy the freedom of democracy, but this time they do so with a different consciousness. The women have not forgotten the empowerment they gained when they learned they could change things by taking to the streets and protesting the dictatorship, and they take this new confidence with them as they face Chile's problems of today.

FEDEFAM is one women's group that has remained particularly active in the new government. This group pressures the Alwyn administration to force the military to explain what happened to and to account for the disappeared.

Nevertheless, women's participation on a formal level in the government continues to be minimal. Alwyn's government has not named any women ministers, only three senators, six representatives, and three sub-secretaries to the House of Justice and to the Ministry of Natural Resources. At this moment, the principal goals of women's groups are the nomination and election of women to public offices, modifying the constitutional articles that discriminate against women, and the establishment of a Ministry for Women.

CONCLUSION

Women's coordinated efforts won them the right to vote but that their solidarity was fragile; class differences curbed cooperation among them after their victory. Nevertheless, with incorporation into the political arena, women began to vote regularly and to affiliate with political parties—albeit male dominated and male-oriented parties. The conservatism engendered by this affiliation was shattered, however, by the authoritarian government of Pinochet. Women became feminist political actors and created new ways of doing politics.

It is difficult to think or theorize about how politics for and by women are made. Kirkwood suggests, however, that:

> To document the political, feminist demands is to demonstrate the existence of this other form of legality, of that counter-power, and why not, of that strength that constitutes the women's attempt to achieve their own liberation. It is to show that it does not matter how far or how near we have been to achieving it without visibility. And it is also to demonstrate the transformation of the members of a specific social group that has not been completely identified as

such by either the outsiders or by the group members themselves, and who, up to now, have only been at the receiving end of good or bad policies implemented to benefit their alleged humanity.

Pinochet emphasized women's role as mothers and developed programs specifically designed to reinforce their traditional position. The Mothers' Centers established by Allende, for example, were strengthened by Pinochet in order to help women care for their domestic responsibilities. But this assistance came with a significant measure of political indoctrination, the goal of which was to discourage women's political activism. Chilean women, however, victims of political repression, were not to be discouraged. And, ironically, they began their attack against authoritarianism by using the very role of mother stressed by Pinochet.

They argued that the State had stolen their children, thereby violating established ethical principles. Uniting under the banner of human rights, women went into the streets to demand the return of their loved ones. They began creating new ways of doing politics, a politics based on moral principles of justice and non-violent struggle. And they imbued their actions with a feminine creativity that expressed itself in the creation of *arpilleras*.

In the view of the state, women became subversive mothers. They did not take the role of the traditional domestic-sphere mother, but assumed that of the publicly-dissenting revolutionary mother. The fascist government's view of women as mothers, guardians of the nation and its children, was rejected by women. Their actions constituted an act of negation of the traditional value associated with the mother roles as well as a desire to emerge under a new banner: that of political mothers, not solely reproductive mothers.

The women's groups organized during the Pinochet regime were responses to authoritarianism; they were alternate forms of uniting and of creating a means of participation in a situation in which all other avenues to act politically were closed. Organizations dedicated to human rights were at the forefront, coordinating the actions of the different groupings. They united political action with human rights, forming numerous coalitions to support the needy, in particular, and the country, in general.

These women continued to speak out against social injustice on the basis of their relationship as mothers to sons and daughters. While their roles as feminists was still unclear, a feminist conscience slowly began to awaken in these women as a specific negation of authoritarianism. And this consciousness allowed them to recognize the relationship between democracy in the country and democracy at home.

When these women met to plan and devise strategies, the hierarchies and traditional forms of conducting politics disappeared; the members sat at round tables, the discourse became personal, and the conversation turned to the private spaces of the home and to women's relationships with husbands and sons. The women's purpose was to reform the private as well as the public domain. Through a process of introspection, they analyzed the role historically assigned to women as well as ways to change the structures that buttressed this practice.

Traditionally-assigned codes (e.g., mother/nurturer) began to disappear and new ones (e.g., activist/dissenter) emerged that were united in the following combination: women and politics. Women's struggles culminated in the triumph of the democratic government headed by Patricio Alwyn. Their victory was due largely to the union established among them. Women from a range of backgrounds and affiliations agreed that without democracy there could be no feminism.

Paradoxically, the rebirth of the feminist movement in Chile was born under the yoke of authoritarianism. During the Pinochet regime, women occupied the territories previously forbidden to them, and they transformed these spaces into forums in which their voices could be heard. Streets were lit up, rallies were organized, and women invented new ways to march in the public spaces. Tired of their lack of expression within political parties and the regimentation of the left and right, women began to occupy these political territories in an audacious way. And as they began to think politically, they began to formulate strategies to achieve new identities.

Women's actions, according to Kirkwood, were not about the search for theoretical definitions, such as "feminist" or "liberated" woman. Rather, the women identified particular obstacles (such as the dictatorship) and then concentrated on strategies and tactics to bring about change. Each women's group thought about what to do in order to mobilize, though sporadically and through symbolic invocations, the majority of women toward the policies of their respective political parties.

The women's actions represented a search for answers to specific questions: how are politics made by and for women? Once women defined "what to do," they were able to think about ways to undermine the subjective and objective obstacles which obstructed the formulation of new policies and their realization.

According to Kirkwood, neither democracy nor feminism can exist within the context of authoritarianism. The only avenue available to women under the Pinochet government, then, was to mobilize in opposition to the regime. The problems of women's discrimination were secondary to this aim, and they could be addressed only later or only if they did not stand in the way of the primary goal: defeating the authoritarian regime.

Chilean women transformed the political process with their moral stance and feminine creativity. Within an authoritarian regime, power is an absent force. Power works from the outside, it invents an alternate strategy based on ethical concepts, collective morals, and adherence to human rights. Women discovered their power during the Pinochet dictatorship. They became political agents rather than appendages to men in politics. Chile is now undergoing a transition toward democracy. These changes offer women new possibilities for articulation and incorporation within and outside the state. The experiences accumulated during the years of the dictatorship will serve as a new and different platform on which women conduct politics by and for themselves. These experiences represent a rupture with old party divisions and create new spaces for women, spaces where they can learn about and prepare for their future inclusion in the different arenas of government.

THE DANCE OF LIFE
WOMEN AND HUMAN RIGHTS IN CHILE

During the seventeen years of military dictatorship in Chile, women formed the country's most visible human rights groups.[1] In times of severe repression and censorship, many women dared to enter a forbidden zone: the streets. From this space—which was previously considered a male domain—these women demanded justice and truth concerning the fate of their loved ones who were missing due to state-sanctioned terrorism.

It is a paradox that, during the periods of worst repression in the 1970s and 1980s, Latin American women took on new roles. Accustomed to living in the confined spaces of the home and other historically female places such as markets, schools, and hospitals, through public protest women broke out of their physical isolation to transform their traditional, apolitical, passive role.

Women's language is intimate and personal, a discourse full of nurturing elements. Nevertheless, under the dictatorship in Chile, as under other dictatorships in Latin America, women transformed their language to address the political repression taking place in the country. They went out into the streets to make their voices heard, because that is where individuals become visible, movements are born, history unfolds, and authority is exercised. Women transformed the "masculine" streets through the use of uniquely female symbols, such as the handkerchiefs embroidered with the names of missing children used by the Mothers of Plaza de Mayo in Argentina. As Adriana Valdes points out, the mothers thus decontextualized and reinterpreted the language of the street.[2]

The mothers' traditional role in society legitimized their search for an answer to the disappearance of their children. The women's unique strategy in denouncing the violations of human rights served as an opening to the public space of the street and to history. Through activities charged with a profound cultural symbolism, such as marching every Thursday afternoon in a plaza in Buenos Aires, the Mothers of Plaza de Mayo occupied the public space that was previously denied to them as women.

The authoritarian ideology paradoxically permitted them to create a collective female space and a uniquely female set of images. The women filled the physical, historical, public space with a plethora of messages: the photographs of the faces of young people tied to their mothers' chests, the white, embroidered kerchiefs bobbing on the women's heads in beat with their steps. Through this strategy, the Mothers of Plaza de Mayo created for themselves, as well as for those who observed them, different images and ways to unmask the oppressive military regime. They did this through and from a woman's perspective.

In the case of Chilean women, the strategy of unmasking the oppressors has also been powerful. One of these strategies has been the symbolic transformation of the *cueca,* the national dance of Chile, into the *cueca sola*—the *cueca* of solitude.

On March 8, 1983, various groups of Chilean women that were fighting against Pinochet's fascism met to celebrate International Women's Day. Signs and banners filled the Caupolican Theater, located in the center of Santiago. A large sign proclaimed "Democracy in the country and in the home," underscoring that the personal is political and that domestic violence is profoundly linked to the violence in the country as a whole. The most memorable event that afternoon was the performance of the *cueca sola,* an important symbol created during Pinochet's dictatorship. Although Chile is now a democracy, women continue to dance the *cueca sola* at public demonstrations to demand justice from the government.

The *cueca* symbolizes the different stages of a romantic interlude between a man and a woman. As the guitar and harp intone the melody and hands joyously clap the rhythms, the man lifts his head, raises his large kerchief, and smiles. Face to face a few steps apart, the couple's movements unfold around an imaginary circle.[3]

The *cueca sola* is danced alone by a female member of the Association of the

Detained and Disappeared The performance suggests a strategy of revealing oneself before the oppressive power as well as appropriating the language of the body in a public space. The audience is quite familiar with the *cueca*, since it is the national dance and appreciates the irony of the fact that it represents the same nation that has deprived the dancer of her children.

The *cueca sola* has become an important metaphor for Chilean women confronting human rights violations. Popular culture has noted and incorporated these acts of remembrance in honor of the missing, where members of the Association of the Detained and Disappeared perform a dance of loneliness and lost love in front of an emotional crowd.[4] International music stars have been inspired to write songs about this ritual, including Sting's "They Dance Alone" and Holly Near's "Hay una mujer desaparecida."

Judith Lynne Hanna, in her book *Dance, Sex and Gender,* notes that women's dances are an affirmation of their identity. Addressing the importance of female dance at the beginning of the twentieth century, she states:

> Through modern dance and its affirmation of the female body, women choose to be agent rather than object. Constrained economically as well as physically by male-imposed dress styles that distorted the body and hampered natural movement, by restricting education, and by health practices that prevented them from breathing fresh air and eating a sensible diet, some innovative women displayed their strength and their displeasure with traditional roles by breaking the rules of the rigidly codified traditional ballet. They extended the boundaries of dance with revolutionary movement vocabularies, grammars, composition techniques, themes, and costumes. Women offered new dance systems and images alongside the *danse d'ecole* developed by men. Showing their new choreography onstage invited audience admiration, empathy, and contact, perhaps relieving some women's male-imposed feelings of social and physical insignificance.
>
> The dance medium also permitted women to control and sublimate their sexuality, which had been dominated by men. To get ahead in an uncharted avant-garde, some women needed a nun-like dedication; other middle- and upper-class respectable women

in dance had love affairs in and out of marriage to show their new sense of social/sexual equality.[5]

A woman who dances alone evokes in the *cueca*'s rhythm the memory of the man who is absent, and the dance changes from a pleasurable experience to a well of pain and memory. The woman's kerchief reminds the spectator of the shrouds that cover a dead body. The woman's steps take on a certain power as she moves alone through an empty stage.

As the country's official national dance, the *cueca* is full of a vast symbolism and history. The women attempt to transform and decentralize this "official" status by inverting its historical and political connection with freedom. The *cueca sola* thus becomes subversive and is reborn as a metaphor of repression and a symbol of women who fight for human rights. The dance comes to represent a denunciation of a society that makes the bodies of victims of political violence disappear, denying them a proper burial and a space to occupy, even underground, and silencing their mourners.

Through the *cueca sola,* the dancers tell a story with their solitary feet, the story of the mutilated body of the loved one. Through their movements and the guitar music, the women also recreate the pleasure of dancing with the missing person. When the women step onto the dance floor, they invokes the dead and perform a dance of life for them.

Each act of forced disappearance is a metaphor for all clandestine acts. The *cueca sola* implies a defiance of these illegal acts, but it also represents a social event where rhythms and movements take place that wouldn't be permitted anywhere else.[6] As in the women's demonstrations in the streets, with the *cueca sola,* women take control of public spaces and languages prohibited to their gender and, in turn reinterpret and reinvent official forms of discourse.

The women's commitment to historical and political truth is linked to their personal set of ethics. In dancing the national dance in this way, the group's members denounce the government's actions on the public space of the dance floor. By dancing the national dance of Chile alone, the women begin to emerge as historical beings with an identity of their own, defying the tradition of couples dancing together. The *cueca sola* breaks the protocol of the dominant culture where women are prohibited from dancing by themselves and, symbolically, with their missing, dead loved ones.

In 1983, the Association of the Detained and Disappeared formed a folklore group, where women collectively sing and compose songs about their lives as women alone.[7] Most *cuecas* deal with love and the eternal struggle of a man to win a woman's love. In the *cueca sola*, the woman is the one who searches for the affection of the missing man, who also symbolizes the mutilated and divided country.

Violeta Parra (1918-1967), one of the best-known folklore figures in Chile and throughout Latin America, is remembered and invoked by the women who write and perform the *cueca sola*. Parra sang two types of melodies that later became *cuecas* and that appealed to God and humanity to alleviate the pains of daily life.[8]

The members of the Association of the Detained and Disappeared sing *cuecas* to God, pleading for guidance in their search for the bodies of their loved ones. The women sing in the style of Violeta Parra, imitating her distinctive, rustic voice and guitar. When they sing as a group, they use harps, guitars, and clapping. The *cueca's* rhythms are important; in the case of the *cueca sola*, they echo "where are they?"

Different *cuecas solas* are sung at demonstrations and memorial services, among them "Te he buscado tanto tiempo" (I have searched for you for so long). The song's theme is the search for a missing person, and the lyrics describe a long journey through the country and an accusation of the guilty.

> I have searched for you for so long
> I can't find you
> I have lost, I have cried out
> and no one wants to listen to me.[9]

The powerful chorus reveals the position the family members find themselves in as they search:

> I demand the truth
> I will search heaven and earth
> without tiring of my search
> and I will give my whole life
> and I will give my whole life
> to know where they are.[10]

The last verse of the "Song of Hope" reflects the collective search, the common consciousness in all of the dancers and in all of the women:

> Give me your hand, Maria
> take my hand, Rosaura
> give her your hand, Raquel
> let's affirm our hope.[11]

One of the group's members, referring to the sense of hope that the women share, tells us:

> This hope is based on the strength that the struggle for life gives us. It may be that many of our family members have not survived the atrocities to which they were subjected, but according to the testimony of people who were with them, many could have remained in hidden places, and we still might be able to rescue them.[12]

The dance represents an affirmation of life and a negation of death. In the *cueca sola,* the pleasure of dancing goes beyond the exploration of the music and the movements. Dance, and in particular this dance-remembrance, permits the body to free itself from all bonds. Through the *cueca sola* and its movements full of soft and delicate cadences, the women are representing the free body, the body that hasn't been tortured, the body that is full of life. For this reason, the folklore group is called "Song for Life." It is a life committed to politics and searching, as well as to meeting with women and hearing their individual stories. The disappearance of a loved one becomes part of the country's history, and the concept of homeland assumes a female identity; one of the slogans of the women who fight for human rights is "freedom is the name of a woman." The *cueca sola* recalls the past, the company of a partner, pleasure, desire, and the sensuality of dancing with a loved one. The dance also reflects the pain of missing a loved one:

> At one time my life was blessed
> my peaceful life filled my days

but misfortune entered my life
my life lost what I loved the most
At one time my life was blessed.

I constantly ask myself
where are they keeping you
and no one answers me
and you don't come back.[13]

According to Leslie Godfrid, the vision and passion that the dance inspires can be powerful in promoting social transformation.[14] As a form of resistance and denunciation of the illegal actions of dictatorship, the *cueca sola* reflects this transformational quality.

The creation of *arpilleras* by the families of the detained and disappeared during the years of military dictatorship also represents a form of resistance.[15] *Arpilleras* are small textile collages made from rags that depict daily life. During Pinochet's dictatorship, women whose relatives were kidnapped anonymously embroidered *arpilleras* that recount their personal suffering, as well as the nation's pain. In 1983, the women who created the *arpilleras* went a step further and, in addition to using their hands to embroider, they presented their whole bodies in public protests. The bodies of the persecuted came to life in the bodies of the women who invoked them with their hands, feet, and kerchiefs in the air.

Watching a woman dance the *cueca sola* has a great impact, because her steps reflect the daily trajectory of a murky, national history. We again observe the incredible transformational power of the women who, from within the dominant culture and through this inherently masculine, national dance, created a new, alternative cultural space. The women are truly alone, without men or a country, because this same country has taken away their men, their sons, their husbands, as reflected in the following *cueca sola:*

Ladies and gentlemen
I am going to tell a story
of all I have suffered
and I keep it in my memory.

It is a very sad story
that I would rather not tell you
what happened in my country
where life isn't worth anything.

Children were left without parents
and mothers abandoned
life has been destroyed
the injustice doesn't end.

How sad it is for the children
when their father is missing
they are left with only
their mother's protection.

I want this to end
and that they be punished
for the crime they have committed
with "the disappeared."

And with this I say goodbye
a small piece of crystal
and those who have committed
this crime
must pay with their lives.[16]

Dancing the *cueca sola* is, then, a way for women to overcome the silence and to remember the dead. With the movement of their bodies, they recount what has happened to them, using their roles as mothers and wives to interpret the male language of the street and of history through a female set of images.

The *cueca sola*, and its relationship to resistance and denunciation, is a powerful phenomenon of Chilean popular culture. Many Chilean women have been abused, through torture or domestic violence. The women who dance the *cueca sola* use their bodies and the sensuality of their movements to tell their stories to a captive and compassionate audience, transforming the country's traditional dance into a call for freedom. Women appropriate the symbolism of the *cueca* as they dance for independence, and through this strategy they dedicate their free, whole bodies to the cause:

> Long is the absence
> and throughout the land
> I ask for conscience.[17]

With its powerful and moving symbolism, the *cueca sola* has become one of the most creative and effective forms of protesting human rights violations in Chile. For this reason, the women say as they approach the stage: "We have created this *cueca* as testimony of what we are living and to fight so that a woman will never again have to dance the *cueca sola.*"

Translated by Janice Molloy

REMNANTS

Women are always doing things with their hands. They prepare flour so that no strange particle will sift through its shiny transparency. With knives sharpened by love, they cut glistening umbilical cords, and when the years bring close the rituals of farewell, women bathe the dead. The most sensible and melancholy women make their own funeral shrouds, using the clothing of their loved ones. In the Kentucky flatlands women used to make their shrouds from the patchwork quilts of their loved ones to enable them to meet them on those leaning thresholds of death.

Patchwork is an unusual phenomenon, maybe even more so than love. Without any artistic pretense, women from both the fields and the cities create dazzling, exquisite tapestries. And this is, indeed, all the more astonishing because they are made from leftovers and scraps.

Once I asked my Aunt Luisa to tell me where her remnants had come from, and she said, "From cloth gags, a tailored suit from a single night of love, and a dish towel." She also told me she had hidden away some special love letters which had been written on flour sacks, and from those golden words she had made little square remnants. Do you believe such craziness? Women do patchwork because they are patient and alone. It is how they become the seemingly impossible: a chorus of mutes.

I can assure you that you are not familiar with another kind of patchwork, the sort that is made from the stories of the dead. In a strange country, lost between immense mountain ranges, no one would listen to the women. When they went to the river crying softly, dragging up their dead, no one heard them. So they made up their minds to work with voiceless remnants.

Unexpectedly, but systematically, their husbands stopped coming home. Terror kept these women from walking out to their patios or to the corner of the street to ask if anyone had seen the men. Terror kept them from walking past the cemeteries, which were full of peculiar, nameless bodies. So the women tore up shirts, undershorts, and wedding dresses and took those tiny pearls from the stale pieces of their wedding cakes, and told their stories.

Hence, in those small, lost gardens of perverse cities, when it is possible to observe the mysteries of light, the women are there, silent and torn, and birds grow out of their hands. A few of them tell about when their husbands were taken away. One describes her daughter's first communion dress. Another remembers a window, her wedding dress, sheets upon which she slept with her husband in a narrow bed, folded in each other's arms, anxious and loving one another.

One women creates with scraps of material from the clothing of a man taken away on a stark and descending evening. They didn't have to take him by force. He stood, without his slippers, wearing only his socks, and he left in this way. She is unable to stop making stories out of remnants, and that scene of when they took him away is like a door of smoke. She has asked her neighbor to lend her a piece of gauze for her patchwork to make tiny doors of smoke.

It is said there is another women who makes only heads that fly in the vastness of a park because in her dreams she saw how they chopped her husband's head off, like they do to chickens every Sunday in small towns. That's why she makes only heads, and when she makes them, they roll onto the grass, crying, howling.

The women work alone or in the company of other women. It is said that in the evening they lock themselves in with locks made of fear, and they cry all by themselves in between the outer fringes and the meadows. When the sirens wail, they stop crying because they believe they they, too, will be taken away. And when the evening becomes a silent cloak of stars, they dream about the next day's scraps of cloth. They awaken with a certain sense of peace and contentment. Then they sit alone in the kitchen, or bent over, perhaps, on a small bench in the patio. And they cut the material as if to give a kiss or paint a picture. They draw faces, with bandages and without them. Sometimes they add words: "Why were they taken away?" "Where could they be keeping them?" And they always ask each other if the men might be cold. Now I can see them making huge patchworks with little squares of color, like the colors of love, the pinks of peaches, the reds of watermelons, and I see that each tapestry is splashed with birds and fruits and windows. And with patience, they pronounce the names. And with patience, they ask each other once again if the men might be cold and why they don't come back.

These women always work with tiny things, common things, unwanted things that people threw away. And from those leftovers, they create memory to scare away the cold and to remember love.

Translated by Diane Russell-Pineda

SUMMER IN THE
SOUTHERN HEMISPHERE

It's summer in the southern hemisphere, and a warm brightness permeates the beginning of the days. There is an insinuating aroma of fresh fruit, especially peaches and figs. I returned in December to Chile, my country. It is the fifth year of democratic rule and Chileans are preparing for Christmas holidays. On December 9, the Christian Democrat Eduardo Frei won the presidential elections, assuring democratic stability.

A rhythm of festival is palpable in the air, presaging the new year. Both children and their parents wear colorful garments, and the city seems bedecked in multicolored balloons. It's sumertime in Santiago. However, for the previous government's victims and their families, these Christmas holidays signify rupture, absence, and desertion.

The most visible of these people are women who have remained widows, who have lost loved ones, and whose fruitless search for the disappeared has spanned almost twenty years. They remain steadfast, however, in the face of the pain. They continue the struggle for human rights, affirming that the years of dictatorship must be remembered so that history does not repeat itself.

I can't help but reflect on the changes in the lives of one group of women whom I first met in Chile during the military dictatorship of General Augusto Pinochet (1973-1989) and whom I recently visited. This group of women began in 1974 to create *arpilleras,* patchwork tapestries which denounce human rights violations in the country. Hardly anyone makes these tapestries anymore.

The precarious, almost abandoned, situation of the *arpilleristas* coincides with the state of absolute silence with respect to human rights in Chile today. With the restoration of democratic rule in 1989 under President Patricio Alwyn, Chile entered a phase in which the political mobilization of women in diverse sectors came to a halt. The suspension of the arpillera workshops is simply a microcosm of what has happened to grassroots organizations more generally. Not only human rights but also economic justice go largely undefended today. The democratic government has created an image of economic success and prosperity, while Chileans who live in extreme poverty in the shantytowns have been forgotten.

The history of the Chilean arpilleras runs parallel to the history of the military dictatorship. In 1974, a group of around thirteen women began to run into each other in the same places—morgues, hospitals, and torture centers. They discovered that they shared remarkably similar stories: the detention of children and husbands and, later, the disappeareance of their loved ones. The first arpilleristas were mostly middle-aged mothers in search of their children. This group inspired the birth of other groups in the zones ringing Santiago. I estimate that from 1976 until 1988, thirty-two workshops, whose members varied in age from seventeen to eighty, were active in urban Santiago.

The large majority of these women belonged to the lower middle class. They lived in the popular neighborhoods, where their children were community activists and leaders. This lower middle class, already with few resources, saw its economic position plummet drastically with the advent of dictatorship. "After the coup," says Violeta Morales, one of the founders of the arpillera workshops, "my family lost everything—a pension and two factory jobs. Before we had a shop and we never lacked for food. My mother had jewelry and other valuables that we had to sell; thanks to this, we were able to get by for a time."

Although a small number of arpilleristas were from the upper middle class, class conflicts and social hierarchies dissolved in the arpillera workshops before the common adversity of pain. The women's central concern was political mobilization around the search for their missing children and husbands.

The great force of social transformation gestating in the urban zones of Santiago motivated many of these women to join the workshops. In addition to the arpillera workshops, these women also participated in the creation of communal kitchens and educational groups. They invented strategies to challenge the fear, feed their children, and engage in a new form of political activism and of struggle against authoritarianism.

The Vicariate of Solidarity—an organization created by the Archbishop of Santiago in 1974 to defend against the constant violation of human rights—gave the first group of women a place to gather. These thirteen women, under the wing of the Vicariate, met every week from 1974 to 1989 to tell their stories by means of the *arpilleras*.

The *arpillera* was born spontaneously; there are no antecedents in Chilean popular culture of making tapestries for political denunciation. Using a domestic, essentially feminine tradition of embroidery, the women protested the destruction of their lives and homes, economic scarcity, constant psychological tension, and the fruitless search for family members. At first, their struggle was distinctly maternal: to rebuild family alliances destroyed by the dictatorship, and to find their children. These women, however, developed a broader political mission. Using worn remnants of fabric—even from their own closets—these women subverted the conventional order by means of embroidery that denounced authoritarianism.

The *arpilleras* tell the story of a divided Chile in graphic and visible form. They contain figures immersed in the daily life of a dislocated society. Certain themes recur, such as disappearance, hunger, torture, and the wounded family —a metaphor for a divided country. Scenes of nature—leafy trees, a huge sun, and the Andean mountains framing the countryside—are also common because despite the leitmotif of pain, there is hope.

The *arpillera* is not an adornment; neither is it made to cover oneself or to simply pass the time. The weaving is made for one purpose: to denounce and expose. It has the power to condemn the invisible tortures and clandestine detentions. It brings us closer to memory. It recovers the names of the disappeared, the places that caught their attention, and the spaces they inhabited.

My work with the *arpilleristas* began in 1979, the time of greatest unemployment in the country. Joblessness reached thirty-five percent nationwide and eighty-one percent in the shantytowns where many of the *arpilleristas* lived. I remember meeting with the women in a room in the Vicariate. I was impressed by the solidarity that existed among them, and the care with which they discussed the themes of the *arpilleras*. They spoke eloquently of blankets without bodies to cover and, more than anything, of their immense solitude.

Curiously, in these most difficult years of the military dictatorship, a bold spirit reigned. The women were willing to make sacrfices, united by their common struggles and aspirations. They engaged in dialogues and planned projects.

Through these groups, the women acquired a deep sense of politics. By means of the tapestries, they undertook a collective dialogue grounded in social justice and the commitment to transform an authoritarian culture into a democratic and cooperative one. The impact of these women on the struggle for democracy was enormous. The *arpilleristas* were among the principal aesthetic voices in the struggle to awaken the international community to the horrors of the Chilean political situation.

With the passage of time, the activity of the Chilean *arpilleristas* took on an international dimension. Solidarity groups in Europe and the Americas exhibited their work, bought it, and more than anything, supported the women with social campaigns on their behalf. The renown that this anonymous work gained was almost magical given that it did not have consumer aspirations and was never promoted by mass-marketing strategies. People around the world were genuinely moved by the dignity of this peaceful form of political protest by women whose family lives and economic situations had been tragically violated.

In 1983, the first group of *arpilleristas* also created a folkloric group that tried to use dance to recover an autochthonous culture and to subvert the dominant national identity. They invented the *solo cueca,* a variation on the *cueca,* the Chilean national dance that is normally danced in pairs. The *arpillerista* dances it solo because her *compañero* has disappeared. This dance, rooted in Chilean folkloric tradition, is thus overturned by the image of a woman dancing alone because the body of her loved one is lost.

In the democratic beginning of 1982, the *arpilleristas* forged alliances with other groups against the dictatorship, among them university groups and popular women's organizations. All these groups united to raise their voices in protest against repression. Without doubt, this collective mobilization precipitated the fall of the Pinochet government.

My return to Chile in the first years of democratic rule and then again last December have left me in a state of deep consternation. Despite the initial exhilaration of the 1988 plebiscite in which fifty-seven percent of Chileans voted against the dictatorship and the jubilation of those exiles who returned, another Chile has appeared. This Chile is a product of neo-liberal economics which have geographically segregated people. "The beautiful people" concentrate in the elite neighborhoods of Santiago, while "the others" live in the periphery—the invisible sectors of the city.

In its first year, the Alwyn Administration created an investigative commission to look into the crimes committed by the military government and the fate of the disappeared. Its five-volume report documents the disappearance of more than 2,500 people. The report caused a big commotion in the country and produced a state of collective shock. The news media managed, however, to diffuse the guilt of the regime with reports of the supposed terrorism that the government confronted at the time. And although the commission acknowledged the culpability of the Pinochet government, it did not recommend the trial and punishment of the guilty parties.

What has happened to the extraordinary historic, artistic and symbolic activity in the *arpillera* workshops? The answer is crushing and thoroughly disheartening. With the advent of democracy in 1989, the thirty-two existmg *arpillera* workshops closed. Of the approximately two-hundred women who made *arpilleras* in the urban zones of Chile, only thirteen truly active women remain.

Now, with the passage of nearly twenty-one years since the beginning of the dictatorship, these women have aged. They confided in me that they have lost the desire to "get dressed in the morning," to manage their lives, to be grandmothers. "The dictatorship," says Violeta Morales, "took the possibility of life away from us." Nonetheless, these thirteen regularly meet and maintain among themselves the bonds of solidarity that have unconditionally united them since the first deplorable years of the Pinochet regime. The miracle of free-market economics hasn't touched them.

The Vicariate of Solidarity closed its workshops in 1991, indicating in numerous newspaper articles that it had concluded its work in defense of human rights in this new phase of democracy and reconciliation. The women say that other international bodies—among them the World Council of Churches and Amnesty Intemational—have also withdrawn their support. The *arpilleristas* have been left feeling disillusioned, confused, and morally abandoned. The women associate democracy with the image of a country molded from indifference and pain.

I saw the women arrive at the workshops tired and with worn-out shoes. They told me that their economic difficulties had grown worse because of inflation as well as the lack of *arpillera* sales. Today, the production of *arpilleras* is sporadic. The women only make *arpilleras* when they have orders from foreign countries. In Chile, the sale of *arpilleras* is non-existent.

The end of the Vicariate's support is symptomatic of the general state of silence in the face of what has occurred–a kind of complicity with the years of dictatorship. The Vicariate's decision was also a capitulation to the systematic imposition of the cultural values linked to market capitalism–the exaltation of individual success, order and national security. Curiously, many of these values are carry-overs from the authoritarian model of the previous regime.

It's easy to see why the thirty-two workshops located in the city's periphery disappeared. The women found it almost impossible to continue with communal kitchens and *arpillera* workshops when not only economic aid but also moral support vanished. Those *arpilleristas* who did not lose children but dedicated themselves to the workshops as a way to attack hunger can no longer afford the cost of public transport or the time to organize themselves. Life in Chile for those people concealed in the invisibility of extreme poverty is ever more precarious.

Why have these women who began the *arpillera* workshops in 1974 continued with the work? What makes them different from the rest who have quit making the tapestries? Perhaps the answer lies in the fact that these women are determined that their fruitless search of more than seventeen years will not be in vain. They carry on to demand a certain justice that would vindicate the work of their family members. As many told me, the disappeared children gave their lives for others and "now no one speaks for them."

The *arpilleristas* feel the absence of the women who once belonged to the other workshops. They understand, however, that survival, need for employment, and the absence of solidarity made the workshops disappear. In the scale of priorities, the weaving of *arpilleras* became secondary. The thirteen remaining women, anchored in a collective pain, work from a sense of responsibility. They are repositories of the nation's memory, which is essentially feminine.

The women spoke about the importance of continuing to talk about the deceased, to remember them, to build plazas and cities with their names, and to embroider their lives in the *arpilleras*. The creation of *arpilleras* is woven into the fabric of their lives. But on my recent visit, I saw the women more solitary, stamped by the mark of indifference. Very few people know that they continue to make *arpilleras*. The work is ever more difficult. They have to struggle to get the fabrics, to pay for public transportation, and to find a place to meet.

The vigorous *arpillerista* movement that occupied such a visible space in the 1970s and 1980s seems non-existent today. But not even the neo-liberal economic policies of the past five years can eliminate these women entirely. While they live, their presence is historic; they are the conscience of the country. With their gloomy presence and dark clothing—as if they wore their mourning both outside and inside—these women continue to create *arpilleras*. On some of the *arpilleras* the following is written: freedom, bread and justice. The women leave their weekly meetings to return to their homes in the shanty-towns, where light and water are scarce. Democracy has not improved their standard of living and has subjected them to the deep oblivion of a nation that prefers not to speak about its past.

As I bid farewell to the women, they give me new *arpilleras* inscribed with the same question: Where are they? As they have since I first met them, the women ask me to talk with others about their work. They reiterate that it is necessary to talk about the dead and to reconstruct the past. We are in a "democratic" society, however, and only silence envelopes us. The scent of fresh fruit assures us of the continuity of life, but only for some.

Translated by Diedre McFadyen

ISLA NEGRA

Isla Negra, the fabled home of Chilean poet Pablo Neruda, is not really an island nor is it black. It is a small fishing cove about one hundred miles west of Santiago, nestled between Valparíso and Viña del Mar. In the summer, Isla Negra is inundated by vacationers seeking to escape the nose and smog of Santiago. During that carefree season, many young people fall in love for the first time, reciting Neruda's *Twenty Poems of Love* and carving hearts into the trees. But in March, when Chileans take leave of their sumer homes and students go back to school, Isla Negra recovers its own particular rhythm and its unique spirit. As Neruda recalls in his memoirs, *I Confess That I Have Lived,*

"it is in winter when a strange flowering is dressed by the rains and the green and yellow cold of the blues and the purples."

Through the years, Chilean intellectuals, poets, and sculptors have been attracted to this enchanting land. Chilean singer Violeta Parra built her house on Isla Negra in the 1940s among the wildflowers and the rocks. Pablo Neruda loved, above all things, his home on Isla Negra, a simple house built in early 1938 with stones that grew warmer or colder with the changing seasons. He had several large bells installed in his backyard to announce lunchtime, and it was here that he displayed his eclectic collections of seashells, bottles of different shapes and colors, butterflies, and carousel horses. In this house, Neruda extolled the agate stones, the generous expanse of stones and sand that greet the ocean.

The house...I don't know when this was born in me. It was in mid-afternoon, we were on the way to those lonely places on horseback...Don Eladio was in front, fording the Córdoba stream which had swollen...For the first time, I felt the pang of this smell of winter at the sea, a mixture of sweet herbs and salty sand, seaweed, and thistle.

Much of Neruda's later poetry refers to Isla Negra, where fishermen and intellectuals, carpenters and poets have coexisted for decades. Neruda caputred the harmony of this coexistence in a poem about Rafita, a local carpenter who lives to this day in Isla Negra:

> *"Just as I've always thought of myself as a carpenter-poet, I think of Rafita as the poet of carpentry. He brings his tools wrapped in newspaper under his arm and unwraps what looks to me like a chapter and grasps the worn handles of the hammers and rasps, losing himself in the woood. His work is perfect."*

Neruda often invited young poets to his house near the sea. He listened to them with prudence, aware that the gift of his company would reveal itself in their future writings. The poets congregated around the big round table, surrounded by colorfully painted plates and enormous blue bottles, in the company of exquisite Chilean wine and living poetry. For hours on end, they could be heard speaking of different poets, and of the sighs, laments, and first loves immortalized in verse.

My family had a home in Isla Negra, and as a child it was a magical place for me. My childhood was filled with long weekends walking arm-in-arm with my mother along the shores of Isla Negra, learning the textures of each rock and the violence of the moss. From a great distance, I would often glimpse the enormous figure of Don Pablo Neruda wering a red Araucanian poncho, furiously writing with a pencil the color of the turquoise glaciers. It was then that I decided that I liked the vocation of poetry and that few tools were necessary: a green pencil, a piece of paper, the immense ocean for self-affirmation, and perpetual astonishment.

This was Chile in the late 1960s and early 1970s. The country was swept up in a poetic effervescence during which the great poets of the day—Pablo Neruda, Gonzalo Rojas, Enrique Lihn, Nicanor Parra, Delia Domínguez—created their most memorable texts. This paralleled the effervescence of the Popular Unity years, when Salvador Allende (1970-73) tried to bring socialism to Chile through democratic means. Allende's government founded an editorial house, Quimantu, which published popular editions of Chilean and Latin American poetry at prices that everyone could afford. Poetry became part of daily life in Chile. Poetry readings became common in high schools, universities, and trade-union meetings. Other artistic forms also blossomed, such as the colorful murals that lit up Santiago's walls.

Neruda was intensely involved in this unique experiment. His poetry expressed his preoccupation with the social history of his country and the future of its workers, women, and children. Neruda wanted to compose a poetry of simplicity that could be understood by all Chileans.

After the military coup in 1973, which brought Augosto Pinochet to power, Neruda died—some say of a broken heart—and his house in Isla Negra was shut down. For nearly two decades, Chile was subsumed by the violence of silence and censure. Gagged and dressed in mourning clothes, Neruda's abandoned house stood as a symbol of the fate of Chilean poetry under the military regime. Poetry, like Neruda's bells, was forced into silence. The voice of the poet, like the voice of the nation, had been usurped. It is no accident that Allende's death, the military coup in Chile, and the death of Pablo Neruda coincided, marking the end of one of the most lyrical and visionary eras in Chilean culture.

Book prices skyrocketed during the Pincohet years. Poetry recitals and theater performances were heavily censured. Familiar texts of Latin American poetry could not be found in any bookstore, with the occasional exception of selected works of Gabriela Mistral that reinforced the stereotype of her as a teacher and left out references to her political activism. To speak of Neruda was dangerous. Along with singers Violeta Parra and Victor Jara, he was considered a traitor in Pinochet's Chile. The closing of Neruda's house coincided with a clamping down on all public poetry events.

During the years of the military dictatorship, Isla Negra became a deserted and disdainful place where hungry dogs and drunkards singing to themselves roamed the dark streets together. Neruda's house, which once hummed with the rhythm of love and the seasons, remained anchored in an unconquerable undergrowth of briers that could not be removed even by the most able of gardeners. A huge sign read "House Closed, Visits Prohibited." Many people, however, disobeyed and made secret pilgrimages to the island. When they arrived at Neruda's house, they read his poetry out loud and recited the long list of names of the disappeared. They lit candles of hope on Pablo's birthday and that of his wife, Matilde. The most daring pilgrims scribbled love poems onto the wooden fence that surrounded the house. On special occasions, like Pablo and Matilde's wedding anniversary, the fences were filled with red flowers.

Since Chile's return to democracy in 1990, artistic and cultural activities have been resurrected from the silence imposed by the military. Isla Negra has become once again the country's cultural center. It is in full bloom, like a bride wrapped in orange blossoms. Neruda's house has been reopened. The red train car rests in front of the garden, and the huge bells sound again, harmonizing with the sea. Visitors are now free to walk about Neruda's house and its grounds. Schoolchildren sit with their notebooks, learning happily about the poet's collection of butterflies and shells. If any place in Chile radiates the peace of democracy and the sense of social commitment that characterized the myth of Pablo Neruda and his poetry, it is without doubt the poet's house on Isla Negra, its key lying on the sand:

I lost my key, my hat, my head! The key came from Raul's general store in Temuco. It was outside, immense, lost, pointing out the general store, "The Key" to the Indians. When I came north, I asked Raul for it, I tore it from him, I stole it in the midst of fierce and stormy winds. I carried it off toward Loncoche on horseback. From there the key, like a bride dressed in white, accompanied me on the night train.

I have come to realize that everything I misplace in the house is carried off by the sea. The sea seeps in at night through keyholes, underneath and over the tops of doors and windows.

Since by night, in the darkness, the sea is yellow, I suspected, without verifying, its secret invasion. On the umbrella stand or on the gentle ears of Maria Celeste, I would discover drops of metallic sea, atoms of its golden mask. The sea is dry at night. It retains its dimension, its power, and it swells, but turns into a great goblet of sonorous air, into an ungraspable volume that rid itself of its waters. It enters my house to find out what and how much I have. It enters by night, before dawn: everything in the house is still and salty, the plates, the knives, the things scrubbed by contact with its wildness lose nothing, but become frightened when the sea enters with its cat-yellow eyes.

That is how I lost my key, my hat, my head.

They were carried off by the ocean in its swaying motion. I found them on a new morning. They are returned to me by the harbringer wave that deposits lost things at my door. In this way, by a trick of the sea, the morning has returned to me my white key, my sand-covered hat, my head—the head of a shipwrecked sailor.

Book presentations are celebrated in Neruda's home to enthuiastic audiences, and the house itself has become one of the country's most popular museums. Psychiatrist Luis Weinstein and poet Paz Molina are promoting poetry workshops that bring together artists and local residents to talk and to write poems about the environment. Children from Isla Negra and neighboring areas also meet weekly for these poetry workshops, which have a true communitarian spirit.

Two recently-formed foundations support these and other cultural activities. The Cultural Corporation, which includes intellectuals, teachers, and fishermen from Isla Negra, was established in 1990 to promote artistic activity. The Neruda Foundation was founded in 1989 by personal friends of Pablo Neruda who wanted to preserve the poet's artistic legacy, his manuscripts, and his homes. The Neruda Foundation sponsors a bi-annual cultural magazine, appropriately named *Isla Negra*, that publishes diverse genres of writing, from essays on the environment to love poems. The first issue of the magazine was published in the summer of 1994 and was presented at the well-known Poet's Cafe. With Chilean wine flowing and Neruda's spirit present, someone recited Neruda's moving poem, "The Sea":

The sea tumbles down like an ancient fighter
What is happening there below?
tomatoes, tunnels, tons of lightning, towers and drums.

For me, returning to Isla Negra means returning to the places and things that Neruda loved so much, such as the figureheads from ships' bows that he collected, especially one from the María Celeste that *"was made of dark and perfectly sweet wood."* Visiting Isla Negra means encounters with the seaweed, with the delirious ocean, and with men and women interested in preserving their community.

The place's cultural activities have blossomed in a welcome challenge to the blind consumerism that took hold during the dictatorship and has prospered under Chile's new democracy. Poetry writing has gained new adherents among young people on the island, even though the literary critics only comment on religious poetry or the classics or the poets currently in fashion. Isla Negra continues to celebrate poetry, even though books are extravagrantly expensive and poetry collections are published only on commission.

Literature in Chile today is measured not by its quality but by its market potential. Book publishers prefer facile texts, flighty tales of rumor and intrigue, and other such precarious and fragile material. Dialogue about literature and politics, about eroticism and women, about history and national identity, remains buried in the annals of silenced memory. The enriched life of the Popular Unity years—that sometimes bordered on euphoria—has been forgotten. In Chile today, people don't talk to each other very much and they visit each other even less, allowing the hospitality that characterized Chileans to slip into history. Chile's democracy is compromised by the continuing power of the military. Solidarity is a rare occurence, and "marketing" is the catchword of the day.

Isla Negra is an oasis in a dark and confusing post-coup history of consumerism, cellular telephones, and huge shopping malls. The consumerist frenzy has propagated an image of Chile as an economic miracle, designed for international consumption to attract foreign investors. But it is a Chile that exists under the prism of the diluted colors of abundance, a Chile that during the military regime lost it identity, its character, its culture. Some of that identity is being recreated today on Isla Negra, where, after years of exile, the presence of Pablo Neruda has returned to occupy the central place it deserves. The cove's residents—its poets, its fishermen, its students—celebrate the right to sing, to speak, to reclaim their roots, and to remember Neruda. On Isla Negra, the island of poets, a spirit of future and of new beginnings permeates the crisp ocean air.

Translated by Jo-Marie Burt

LETTER FROM CHILE

I return to my country, Chile, in the month of December. It is summer in the southern hemisphere—the season of peaches and glorious watermelons immortalized in the odes of Pablo Neruda.

The citizens of this nation hidden between the Andean mountain range and the sea are preparing for the end-of-the-year festivals, investing the city with the spirit of multicolored balloons and sales of the traditional holiday flower, a red carnation surrounded with sweet basil.

Although there is an effervescence in the air, it is possible to discern the economic uncertainty of the four million Chileans who live in extreme poverty. In this season of gift buying and holiday spirits, salespeople fill the streets of the big cities. Through the presence of these street vendors, it is possible to observe the poverty of the marginal and indigent, of those who belong to the "other" Chile, far removed from the shining shopping malls and the economic success of a minimal number of Chileans.

The Pinochet dictatorship postulated economic success, and this philosophy continues in the democratic government of Eduardo Frei, who was victorious in the presidential elections on December 9, 1993.

There is no doubt that democracy in Chile has dignified the life of its citizens. The high voter turnout for the presidential elections illustrates the civic and democratic spirit that once characterized this nation as the England of South America The new president, himself the son of a president, must continue the legacy left by the Pinochet years and must above all acknoweledge the presence of the relatives of the disappeared, who continue to demand justice and truth about the fate of their loved ones.

Human rights are not part of the popular discourse of the present democratic government nor were they part of the transitional government of President Alwyn. One senses that the desire to forget the presence of the victims of the years of repression is a constant in the daily experience of the citizenry. However, the relatives of the disappeared continue the symbolic search for their loved ones and continue to anoint their plazas and mausoleums with the names of the disappeared as they endeavor to sustain the memory of their lives.

On August 9, 1993 a hunger strike of one hundred hours was staged next to the Tribunal of Justice by the Mothers of the Disappeared to prevent an Amnesty Law that would grant impunity to the perpetrators of crimes against citizens. Remembering is a constant pursuit for the relatives of the victims, as it is for the writers and the artists who create perpetual remembrance through their works.

The young poet Raul Zurita's verse, "No more pain or fear" stands in the middle of the Atacama desert. Part of a gigantic sculpture, it that represents a unique tribute to the many writers who continue to rethink and recreate the legacy of Pinochet. Writers like José Donoso and Jorge Eduards continue to inspire a generation of younger Chilean authors who create highly symbolic texts haunted by the memory of the dictatorship and its daily presence. The proliferation of workshops attests to the importance of literature in Chilean culture as well. The poetry workshops that flourish throughout the country are numerous, as if the grief and fear could be exorcised by words.

It is summer in Chile; couples kiss in the parks. Yellow and fuchsia flowers cover the fields; fresh fruit stands proliferate along the roadsides, testaments to the generosity of the earth.

Here one breathes a fresh and promising air and the presence of a future beneath a firmly-rooted democracy where there is no more grief or oblivion, where there is no silence or censorship, but only a dialogue of voices that begin to listen to one another with the hope of a new life.

Translated by Celeste Kostopulos-Cooperman

ENDNOTES

THE DANCE OF LIFE: WOMEN AND HUMAN RIGHTS IN CHILE

1. For more information about women and human rights groups in Latin America, see Jean Jaquette, *Women's Protest Movements in Latin America,* Unwin Hyman, 1989.

2. See Adriana Valdes's article, "Mujeres entre culturas," *Revista de critica cultural,* No. 1, Ano 1, mayo 1989, p. 34.

3. This description of the Chilean *cueca* was given by Rodriguez Arancibia, *La cueca chilena–coreografia y significado de esta danza,* Servicio Nacional de Turismo, Santiago de Chile, 1945, p. 42. The most complete book about the *cueca* was written by Pablo Garrido, Editorial Univ., Santiago, Chile, 1980.

4. The Association of the Detained and Disappeared was created in Chile in 1974 by the Vicaria de Solidaridad to investigate the fate of the detained and missing. For more information about this group's work, see the reports by the Vicaria de Solidaridad for 1978 to 1984. This information is available through Vicaria de Solidaridad, Plaza de Armas 444 2do piso, Santiago, Chile.

5. From Judith Lynne Hanna's book, *Dance, Sex and Gender,* University of Chicago Press, 1988, p. 132.

6. "Women Dancing Bach," by Leslie Godfrid, in *Postmodernism, Feminism and Cultural Politics,* edited by Henry A. Simoux, State University, New York Press, 1990, p.178.

7. For more information about the folklore group created by this association, see *Canto por la vida, Agrupacion de Detenidos y Desaparecidos,* Vicaria de Solidaridad, Santiago de Chile, 1987.

8. For more information about Violeta Parra, see Agosin and Dolz, *Violeta Parra– santa de pura greda,* Editorial Planeta, 1988.

9. From *Canto por la vida,* "Te he buscado tanto tiempo," p. 29. This *cueca* was composed by Richard Rojas.

10. *Canto por la vida,* p. 29.

11. *Canto por la vida,* "Cancion de la esperanza," p. 23.

12. *Canto por la vida,* p. 23.

13. "La cueca 8018," collective song in *Canto por la vida,* p. 7.

14. See "Women Dancing Bach," p. 184.

15. For more information about the history of the Chilean *arpillera* movement, see Marjorie Agosin, *Scraps of Life,* Red Sea Press, New Jersey, 1987.

16. *Canto por la vida,* "Una historia," p. 35.

17. From the introduction to *Canto por la vida.*

VISION AND TRANSGRESSION: SOME NOTES ON THE WRITING OF JULIETA KIRKWOOD

1. Published originally under this title in 1986 with the subtitle: *Las feministas y los partidos* (*Feminists and Political Parties*). A second edition, published in 1990, carries the subtitle suggested by Kirkwood before her death (also in 1986) *Los nudos de la sabiduria feminista* (*The Bonds of Feminist Wisdom*). Quotes in the text are from this edition.

2. FLACSO is the Latin American School of Social Sciences. Each chapter in the book was originally a working paper for FLACSO discussion prepared between 1980 and 1983; chapters III and IV were taken from one paper with the same title as the first edition of Kirkwood's book.

WORKS CITED AND SUGGESTED READINGS

Caffarena, Elena. *Un capitulo en la historia del feminismo.* Santiago, Chile: Ediciones MEMCH, 1952.

Covarrubias, Paz. *El movimiento feminista chileno en Chile: Mujer y sociedad.* Compilacion de Paz Covarrubias y R. Frano, UNICEF, 1978.

Kirkwood, Julieta, *Ser politica en Chile: las feministas y los partidos.* Santiago, Chile: FLACSO, 1986; 2nd ed., *Ser politica en Chile: los nudos de la sabiduria feminista.* Santiago, Chile: Editorial Cuarto Propio, 1990.

Klimpel, Felicitas. *La mujer chilena: el aporte femenino al propreso de Chile.* 1910-1960. Santiago, Chile: Editorial Andres Bello, 1962.

Labarca, Amanda. *Femenismo contemporaneo.* Santiago, Chile: Editorial Zigzag, 1947.

Santa Cruz, Adriana, ed. *Tres ensayos sobre la mujer chilena.* Santiago, Chile:

Editorial University, 1978.

Vergara, Marta. *Memorial de una mujer irreverente*. Santiago, Chile: Editorial Zigzag, 1967.

INHABITANTS OF DECAYED PALACES:
THE DICTATOR IN THE LATIN AMERICAN NOVEL

1. Many studies of Latin American literature have addressed this theme in depth. See Angel Rama, *Los dictadores latinoamericanos* (Mexico: Fondo de Cultura Economica, 1976). Also "Tres Novelas de la dictadura," *Cahiers du Monde Hispanique* 29 (1977): 65-87; and Maria Paley de Francescato, "La novela de la dictadura: nuevas estructuras narrativas," *Revista de Critica Literaria* 9 (1979): 9-109. The most detailed of all the studies is Robert Gonzalez Echevarria, "The Dictatorship of Rhetoric, The Rhetoric of Dictatorship," *Latin American Research Review* 15, 3 (1980): 205-228.

2. There is an extensive bibliography of books about authoritarianism in Latin America and its historical roots. I suggest as a starting point *Authoritarians and Democrats: Regime Transition in Latin America*, eds. James M. Malloy and Mitchell A. Selegson (Pittsburgh: Pittsburgh University Press, 1987).

3. Gabriel Garcia Marquez, *The Autumn of the Patriarch,* trans. Gregory Rabassa (New York: Bard Books, 1976), 7.

4. Lopez Rega was minister of social welfare under Isabel Peron and later formed the Triple A (Alianza Anti-Comunista de Argentina). This terrorist group was responsible for many of the disappearances and tortures during the "Dirty War."

5. Tomas Eloy Martinez, *The Peron Novel,* trans. Asa Zatz (New York: Pantheon Books, 1988), 357.

6. Marta Traba, *Mothers and Shadows,* trans. Jo Labanyi (London Readers International, 1986), 88.

7. Diamela Eltit, *Por La Patria* (Las Ediciones de Ornitorrinco, 1986).

A Dream of Shadows: Writing, Speaking, Becoming

1. *El bordado de la escritura* (The Fabric of Writing)," essays on South American Hispanic poetry.

2. Lispector, Clarice *The Foreign Legion* (Carcanet, 1990) p. 150.

Women, Politics, and Society in Chile

1. Such a withdrawal was not unprecedented, however. The women of the Bellen de Zaraga Center also disbanded when they achieved their objectives.

2. The problem of establishing relationships of equality between women of different classes remains one of the important unresolved issues for contemporary feminists.

3. Beginning in 1976, branches of FEDEFAM were established in other Latin American countries, and the organization continues to hold annual meetings in different countries throughout the region .

4. Although originally made by the members of FEDEFAM, the *arpillera* form of art spread rapidly and many groups grew out of the original one. There are currently approximately thirty-two arpillera workshops in Santiago

5. Other groups of women organized to establish soup kitchens and visits to political prisoners, and their members interacted with those of FEDEFAM on an informal basis to administer such activities. These groups, however, were not as visible as the Association of Relatives of the Detained and Disappeared.

6. Little information exists on the many women's groups that were formed during the last years of the Pinochet regime.

Cities of Life, Cities of Change

1. Beginning in 1974, these associations were formed in Chile, Argentina, Uruguay, Guatemala, and El Salvador. In 1980, they were joined in a common organization called FEDEFAM.

2. For more information on the Chilean *arpilleras*, see Marjorie Agosin, *Scraps of Life: Chilean Arpilleras* (The Red Sea Press, Trenton, N.J., 1987).

3. In Greek mythology, the daughter of Minos and Pasiphae, who gave Theseus a thread to help him find his way out of the Minotaur's labyrinth.

SO WE WILL NOT FORGET: LITRATURE AND HUMAN RIGHTS IN LATIN AMERICA

I would like to thank the Pew Foundation for allowing me to teach a course on the subject of this essay, thus inspiring me to complete the study.

1. For an interesting study on authoritarian governments in Latin America and the transition to democracy, see James Malloy and Mitchell Seligson, *Authoritarians and Democrats: Regime Transition in Latin America* (Pittsburgh: University of Pittsburgh Press 1987. See also Stephen Schwartz, ed., *The Transition from Authoritarianism to Democracy in the Hispanic World* (San Francisco: ICS Press, 1986.)

2. Julio Cortazar, *Argentina: anos de alambradas culturales* (Barcelona, Spain: Muchnik Editores, 1984), 89. See also Julio Cortazar, *Textos politicos* (Madrid, Spain: Plaza y Janes, 1984).

3. For poetry that illustrates this theme, see Claribel Alegria, *Flowers from the Volcano,* trans. Carolyn Forche (Pittsburg: University of Pittsburg Press, 1982); Ernesto Cardenal, *With Walker in Nicaragua,* trans. Jonathan Cohen (Connecticut: Wesleyan University, 1984); Teresa de Jesus, *De Repente,* (Williamantic, Connecticut: Curbstone Press, 1982): Aristoteles Espaha, *Dawson* (Santiago, Chile: Editorial Bruguera, 1974); Pedro Orgambide, *Cantares de las madres de la Plaza de Mayo* (Mexico: Editorial del Fuego, 1983); Volcan, *Poems From Central America* (San Francisco: City Lights Books, 1985).

4 Mario Benedetti, *Pedro y el capitan* (Madrid Alianza Editoria, 1976).

5. Ibid., 34.

6. Ibid., 112.

7. Elvira Orphee, *The Angel's Last Conques,t* trans. Magda Bogin (New York: Bantam Press 1986). In Spanish, *La ultima conquista del angel* (Venezuela: Monte Avila Editores, 1977).

8. Ibid., 14.

9. For a reading on the concept of torture and the idea of the wounded body, see Alaine Scarry, *The Body in Pain, the Making and Unmaking of the World*

(London: Oxford University Press, 1985).

10. For a basic article on women and torture, see Ximena Bunster "Surviving Beyond Fear: Women and Torture in Latin America," in *Women and Change in Latin America,* eds. June Nash and Helen Safa (South Hadley Massachusetts: Bergin and Garvin, 1986).

11. Omar Rivabella, *Requiem for a Woman's Soul* (New York: Random House, 1986);Fernando Alegria, *Coral de querra* (Mexico:Editorial Nueva Imagen, 1979).seealsoFernandoAlegria, *Chilean Spring* (Pittsburg: Latin American Literary Review Press, 1984)

12. Alegría, *Coral de querra,* note 11 above, 39.

13. Ibid., 69.

14. Simone Veil, "Introduction" in *Disappeared: Technique of Terror: A Report for the Independent Commission on International Humanitarian Issues* (London Zed Books, 1986).

15. Jacobo Timmerman, *Preso sin nombre, celda sin numero* (New York Random House, 1981); Alicia Portnoy, *The Little School, Tales oi Disappearance and Survival in Argentina* (Pittsburg: Cleis Press, 1986). For interesting studies on the writer and human rights, see Amnesty International, *The Writer and Human Rights,* (New York: Doubleday, 1983); Lihn, Zurita, Ictus and Radrigan, *Literature chilena y experiencia authoritaria* (Santiago, Chile: Santiago FLACSO, 1987).

16. Timmerman, note 15 above, 6

17. Ibid.. 33.

18. Ibid. 61.

19. Partnoy, note 15 above, 67.

20 Marta Traba, *Conversacion al sur* (Mexico: Siglo XXI, 1981). This book was published in English under the name, *Mothers and Shadows* (London: Readers International, 1981)

21. Ibid., 125.

22 For an excellent critical anthology on testimonial literature in Latin America, see Rene Jara and Herman Vidal, eds., *Testimonio y literatura*

(Minneapolis: Minnesota Institute for the Study of Ideologies and Literatures, 1986).

Z3. Ibid., prologue by Rene Jara.

24. Elena Poniatowska, *La noche de Tlatelolco* (Mexico: Editorial Era, 1971).

25. Patricia Verdugo, *Miedo en Chile* (Santiago, Chile: Ediciones Chile y America, 1984).

26 Armando Valladares, *Against All Hope: The Prison Memoirs of Armando Valladares* (New York Alfred A. Knopf. 1986); Jorge Valls, *Twenty Years and Forty Days: Life in a Cuban Prison* (New York Americas Watch, 1986).

27 Valls, note 26 above.

28 Claribel Alegria, *They Won't Take Me Alive* (London: Readers International, 1986).

29. Manlio Agueta, *A Day in the Life* (New York: Viking Press, 1984).

30. Rigoberta Menchu with Elizabeth Burgos. *I, Rigoberta Menchu* (New York: Shoeken Books, 1984).

31. Ibid., 21.

32. Ibid.

33. Ibid., 28.

34. Ibid., 228.

35. Ibid., 168.

36. Ibid., 281.

THE TRANSLATORS

MONICA BRUNO GALMOZZI, born in Costa Rica, received her B.A. in Spanish from Wellesley College and her M.A. in Spanish Literature from Columbia University. She was assistant editor of *Surviving Beyond Fear: Women, Children and Human Rights in Latin America* (White Pine Press, 1993) and has just completed the translation of a new volume of poetry by Marjorie Agosín.

JO-MARIE BURT is a Ph.D. candidate in political science at Columbia University. She is associate editor of *NACLA Report on the Americas,* a magazine analyzing political trends in Latin America, published bimonthly by the North American Congress on Latin America.

LORI M. CARLSON received an M.A. in Hispanic Literature from Indiana University. A former director of literature at the Americas Society, her most recent books include *Cool Salsa* and *Barrio Street, Carnival Dreams,* both published by Henry Holt and Co. She has taught at Indiana University, Columbia University, and New York University

MARK FRIED has translated several books by Uruguayan author Eduardo Galeano, as well as an oral history of El Salvador's Radio Venceremos (*Rebel Radio,* Curbstone Press). Formerly an editor at *NACLA Report on the Americas,* he presently works for Oxfam-Canada in Ottawa.

CELESTE KOSTOPULOS-COOPERMAN holds a Ph.D. in Hispanic Studies from Brown University. Her translation of *Circles of Madness: Mothers of the Plaza de Mayo* by Marjorie Agosín received an ALTA translation prize in 1993. Her translations frequently appear in magazines and anthologies. She is currently director of the Latin American Studies Program at Suffolk University.

DEIDRE MCFADYEN is the managing editor of *In These Times,* a biweekly news magazine based in Chicago. She was an editor of *NACLA Report on the Americas* from 1991-96.

JANICE MOLLOY is a Boston-area editor and translator. Her translations have appeared in numerous anthologies and publications. She has also translated two books by Marjorie Agosín: *Women of Smoke* and *Mothers of the Plaza de Mayo.*

BARBARA E. PIERCE received her B.A. in Hispanic History and Literature from Wellesley College and her M.A. in Latin American Studies from the University of Texas at Austin. Her translations of Marjorie Agosín's work have appeared in magazines and journals. She currently lives in Berkeley, California.

DIANE RUSSELL-PIÑEDA is a translator, writer and human rights activist. She lived for many years in Mexico City where she worked as a translator and teacher. She currently teaches Spanish translation in Washington, D.C.

RICHARD SCHAAF is the editor and publisher of Azul Editions. He lives in Washington, D.C.

MARGARET STANTON is assistant professor of Spanish and Director of the Latin American Studies Program at Sweet Briar College in Virginia. Her translations of short stories and essays by Latin American authors appear frequently in publications and anthologies.

PAULA M. VEGA GUERRA is a graduate of Wellesley College. She is currently the project coordinator for a research center on political and social studies at the Pontificia Universidad Católica Madre y Maestra in Santo Domingo, Dominican Republic. Several of her translations appear in *These are Not Sweet Girls: Poetry by Latin American Women* (White Pine Press 1995).